Handling Holland

ISBN 90 5594 232 4 / NUGI 661

Handling Holland

A manual for international women in the Netherlands

Janet Inglis – XPAT MEDIA

About the author

Janet Inglis came to Holland, like many expat women, in the wake of her husbands job, in 1987. She has done a number of things since then: run a freelance psychological practice (she is a chartered educational psychologist), contributed regular gardening articles for the BWC magazine, worked in The British School in The Netherlands as Head of Psychology, taught several Open University Psychology courses, had a baby (who is now 9 years old), worked as a trainer in industry, and acted as a careers consultant to international women. She enjoys life in Holland and finds it an easy, relaxed place to be. She and her husband, both Scottish, will eventually retire to the ruined tower house they own on the south west coast of Scotland. She can be contacted on janetinglis@csi.com.

Dedication

For Rose and John

Acknowledgements

With grateful thanks to the 50 women who gave their time so generously and were willing to share their experiences and advice with me and you, the reader. Without them, this book could never have been written.

Contents

Unpaid activities

Introduction

What's it all about?

This book is about being happy in Holland. It's a manual for international women who come here from all over the world as expats, whether as jobseekers, relocated workers, trailing spouses or refugees. This is a book of ideas as well as how-to-do-it details. The ideas are backed up and illustrated by the stories of the 50 women whom I have interviewed for the book. I wrote it because I saw a real need among women who arrive in Holland to find answers to the question, 'what can I do?' and an opportunity for women who have been here for some time to share their experiences and advice.

At the beginning of each chapter are the stories of two very different women – not typical expats, because there is no such thing – that loosely illustrate the theme of the chapter. Throughout the chapters are the shorter stories of other women, along with practical advice on what you might like to do to spend your time in Holland.

The typical expat

There is no such thing. The women in this book don't fall into neat categories, any more than you do, and nor do the other expat women you meet in Holland. They are not 'typical' expats, any more than you are. You may think, when you first arrive in the Netherlands and visit The British or American Women's Club, or go to a parents' welcome meeting at your child's international school, or sleep on a friend's floor until you can find cheap accommodation, that you don't fit in here, that everyone else is different from you. And indeed they are – but not as an amorphous mass. If the first six women you meet seem part of an alien group, go out and meet six more. And six more and six more. We are all individuals with different interests and personalities. You **will** find sympathetic souls out there, but it may take time and patience. And you may find that you form friendships with women whose experiences and outlook are very different from your own. Be open and accepting of strange others – you are unlikely to find a social circle here which mirrors the one you had at home, so look at what is available and adapt yourself to the new experiences.

Most of the women I have interviewed are drawn from my personal circle of friends and acquaintances, yet you could hardly find a more diverse group. That, for me, is one of the great pleasures of living in an international community – the opportunity to make friendships with women one would never expect to encounter at home. (Check out chapter 9 for some suggestions on increasing your social circle.)

What do women who come to live in the Netherlands *do*?

There are almost as many answers to that question as there are international expat women. I have known teachers, lawyers, tax advisers, pilots, artists, university lecturers, secretaries, scientists, musicians, cleaners, librarians, translators, nannies, hairdressers, nurses and psychologists – all working in paid employment in English. Some have come on their own account, having applied for a job from outside the Netherlands, or been relocated here by their company. Some are refugees, hoping to find a better life here than in their home country. Many are 'trailing spouses', here because of their partner's job. I have also known many expat women who cannot or don't want to work, but have found great satisfaction in expanding their horizons through new educational, social or travel opportunities.

Recently, a headline in The Sunday Times caught my eye: *Loneliness led British wife to bomb death*. The article went on to tell the tragic story of an expat woman in Athens who was driven by 'boredom and loneliness' into the embrace of Greek organised crime and who became a gangland enforcer. She died when a bomb, which she was carrying in her car, went off accidentally.

Now, doubtless if you are desperate (and as I read on through the article, it became clear that the poor woman who died had all sorts of problems beyond boredom and loneliness) you could find some drug traffickers or diamond smugglers in Amsterdam to employ you on a dangerous and illegal mission and add some spice to your life. But, really, there should be no need to be either bored or lonely in Holland. There is so much to do and so many opportunities to have a really good social life, if that's what you would like. And if you want a job, there are many legal ones on offer, as well as opportunities to build your own small business.

Some women who come here on account of their partner's job are angry, fed-up and frustrated. They may have left a good job of their own back home. They may not like Holland, or indeed, Europe. But if you have agreed to come – no matter how unwillingly – you might as well do your best to enjoy your stay. Take the advice given to new mothers who find it difficult to love their babies at first – act as if you do. If you can't love Holland, just pretend to for the time being. Go out and visit new places, meet new people and get involved in new activities. Perhaps through your efforts in time you **will** come to love it here. But even if you never do, at least you won't have wasted your time.

In this book I aim to show, through the personal stories of many women I have met, and through lots of down-to-earth, practical advice, that there are many, many choices available for International Women in the Netherlands – probably far more than you ever thought. You may not be able to carry on your career exactly where you left off in your home – or last – country, but there are many doors of opportunity here, ready for you to knock on and push wide open.

Expat women who have been here for a long time emphasise the positive changes that have taken place over the past few years (see Things could be worse, page 24). You can make them work for you.

The women in the book

I interviewed 50 women while researching this book, and all gave their time generously and unstintingly. They range in age, from 18 to 67; in social status, from illegal au pair to international judge; in experience, from 30 years in Holland to a few months. They represent 15 different nationalities, and, of course, 50 views on life. Each is an individual, with her own outlook, set of experiences and expectations. But there is a common thread of practicality and common sense when it comes to the advice they give to women coming to Holland for the first time. Often it is advice they themselves would like to have had. Advice is merely an opinion, which you can choose to ignore, of course – nobody is trying to tell you what you **must** do. But through their stories, these women can at least show you that there are very many different ways of having a wonderful stay in the Netherlands.

See chapter 10 for a concentrated selection of advice, under *Words of Wisdom from the Women themselves*.

As a trailing spouse, you might feel that it is simply not possible to get a good job in your own right. You could be wrong. Two of the women in this book with the most senior jobs (**Hettie**, head teacher of an international high school, and **Ebe**, principal director of a major inter-governmental organisation) spent years of their lives trailing around the world in the wake of their husbands, finding jobs for themselves as and when they could, before coming to Holland.

Don't be intimidated by some of the almost heroic achievements described. Not every woman is going to start up an international business or become a leading expert or senior manager in her field. There are plenty of 'ordinary' achievements, too, here.

Christine, from New Zealand, nicely illustrates the diverse and changing roles that many international women play. At first, she stayed home and devoted herself to her young family when she came in 1980. After three years she found a job in a school, using her teaching qualifications.

When she gave up her job, she did voluntary administrative work for a while, until she found a job which used the new skills she had just learned as a volunteer. While working as an administrator for The Open University she studied part-time for a master's degree, then set up a successful business with her husband, providing training packages for business and industry. In her spare time, she keeps herself fit and healthy swimming, playing golf and ballroom and tap dancing. She has also recently learned to play the guitar and contributed to a Dutch book on cross-stitch samplers! (Christine's full story is at the start of chapter 6).

'If you are to make the most of your Dutch experience it's important to consciously immerse yourself in Dutch life, culture and especially the language. Accept that learning a foreign language as an adult is difficult – but don't give up.'

Not all women who come to Holland are middle-aged, middle-class professionals with a residence permit and the right to seek work. Some are refugees and some are here illegally, trying to find a means of support for themselves.

Maria came to Holland from Poland for a kind of unofficial GAP year between school and college, hoping to improve her English. (Why Holland? Because England and the USA are considerably more difficult to enter without full documentation.) She was lucky to find a kind and welcoming English family to employ her as an au pair, through a church network, but both she and the family are concerned that her status in

Holland is not legal. This is not from want of strenuous effort on both their parts. It seems that the process of gaining a one-year residence permit, even with the support of a potential employer in Holland, from countries such as Poland, is hemmed in by a maze of Kafkaesque regulations which make it virtually impossible to obtain the correct papers in the right order. Unemployment in Poland is high and many young Polish people are here working illegally. Obviously, the situation will change if and when Poland enters the EU, but until then Dutch immigration practices do not make things easy for them.

All of the personal stories are true. Most of the names are real names, with the few exceptions where I have been asked not to disclose an identity. The women's personal stories loosely illustrate the chapter headings. But most could fit equally well under other headings, because their lives have so many facets.

The sections

The book is organised in two sections, **paid work** and **unpaid activities**, each part full of practical suggestions and illustrated with the stories of women who have done something special in that area. The ideas for job-search activities, business opportunities, courses, clubs and societies, things to do, etc. are not at all exhaustive. They are there to whet your appetite and to help and inspire you to look further. There is a wealth of information out there in the community and this book can help you to access it, if you use the ideas as a springboard to go on and look further yourself.

Paid work

If you do not go out to work, you may not be aware that many expat women have jobs. Of the 50 women I interviewed, 19 (38%) work for an organisation, and a further 22 work freelance or run a business of their own. These women may not be representative of the expat population as a whole, but over 80% of them are earning money one way or another. Of those women who do work for an organisation, a large majority works in the traditionally female areas of education and office administration.

This is probably partly because there are so many opportunities to work in English. The international inter-governmental organisations, such as OPCW and EPO, the international schools and the international companies, such as Shell, are all big employers of expat women. Increasingly, though, women are working in IT and Telecom, areas where there is currently a shortage of skilled workers. If you can obtain a work permit – and if you are an accompanying partner and/or an EU national, this should be possible – you will almost certainly be able to find a job working in English quite quickly. Your ideal job may take a little longer, but may also be possible. If you are not eligible for a work permit, you can still work if you set up a business – see Robin's story (chapter 1) and Julia's story (chapter 9).

'I like international teaching, although the job can be tedious and hard work at times, especially with two young children. But I like the independence and the practicality of having my own money and feeling able to spend it on whatever I like without even discussing it.'

Working may not be an easy option, especially with children at home, and may not even be financially necessary, but for many women it represents a kind of freedom which is not available through any other means.

Rachel works as a senior lecturer at the prestigious Institute of Social Studies, which is allied to Utrecht University. 'I like international teaching, although the job can be tedious and hard work at times, especially with two young children. But I like the independence and the practicality of having my own money and feeling able to spend it on whatever I like without even discussing it.'

Unpaid activities

Within this section are seven chapters:

- Serving the community
- Expanding your horizons
- Fit and healthy
- Home and family
- Culture and creativity
- Finding friends and having fun
- Decisions, dilemmas and words of wisdom

Obviously, these sections are not mutually exclusive. You may want to have loads of fun while an expat, but also to give something back. There's nothing stopping you from whooping it up at the discos at night and doing volunteer work during the day. Or taking on a paid job and devoting yourself to your family for the rest of the week. Most women will find they fall into several categories. So, dip in for ideas as the need arises and the fancy takes you.

Starting off and settling in

Rosalind's story

Rosalind, co-founder of Formula Two Relocations, came to Holland in 1975, 'as a typical trailing spouse. My husband wanted the experience to work outside the UK, and I was happy to move even though I had to give up a job in London, which I loved, working with an agency which tackled racial discrimination. Much to my surprise, I became very depressed when I came here, despite having a lovely apartment in the centre of Amsterdam. Looking back, I was suffering from culture shock, but in those days the term 'culture shock' was not particularly known.'

Resourceful from the start, Rosalind found herself a couple of secretarial jobs, simply by contacting companies she found from a listing from the British Chamber of Commerce. Within a year of living in Holland her first child was born and a shortly after, her second child. Rosalind stayed at home while they were little, doing some part-time market research for a British consumer organisation investigating new products on the Dutch market.

In 1983 Rosalind met another British expatriate, they became close friends and decided to set up a relocation business together. Rosalind researched the services available to international expats and they launched their relocation business, slowly creating a market for the services they offered. Rosalind marketed the new company by telephoning newspapers to publicise the idea of relocation services, which in 1983 was a virtually unknown concept. Each woman invested Dfl. 500 ('It seemed like an absolute fortune at the time') and they acquired a typewriter and some headed notepaper. For the first two years they worked from home, doing everything between them, investing any income they earned back into the business. After countless hours of cold calling, Hewlett Packard gave them a contract and their business started to take off. 'There's no secret about it,' Rosalind says. 'It was pure hard slog getting clients. In the early days there were many periods when we had no work. But we were in the right place at the right time and companies came back to us because we were good and we were very service-oriented.'

Rosalind and her partner also organised conferences on relocation, not only to publicise their company but also to highlight the need for relocation services. In 1989, they won the title of Marketer of the Year from The American Netherlands Chamber of Commerce and around that time they employed their first relocation consultant. In 1992 they moved from their home office to an office in the Vondelkerk in Amsterdam, which they felt to be an enormous – and very scary – step. The company developed until it became a major force in the relocation business in Holland. In 2001 the two partners split up, Formula Two was closed and Rosalind founded her own independent business, Tristar Relocations with two partners, both ex-Formula Two. Both Rosalind and her partners are looking forward to developing their new company in the years ahead.

Rosalind has helped countless women who have relocated and she has a stack of sound advice to give to women about to come to Holland. 'Do your homework before you come. Ask questions, especially of your employers. Take charge of your own relocation and take advantage of all the information available. Let professionals guide you, because nothing truly prepares you for the reality of relocation. Also, look at yourself and your relationships. Relocation is very stressful and if relationships are not stable, the chances are that the pressures of a move will increase problems, so be honest with yourself and your family; remember you have to uproot yourself not only physically but mentally. Living in a new country, experiencing its culture, making new friends is a wonderful experience. At times it can be daunting, but if you keep an open mind, a sense of humour and are prepared to see the other person's point of view, you will find that you and your family will invariably gain and grow from the experience.'

Dina's Story

Dina is a young Brazilian musician who came to Holland in 1993 to study recorder music for a year at the Rotterdam Conservatorium. 'I never intended to stay long-term, but every year I stayed one more year. Standards of recorder playing are very high in Holland – people come from all over the world to study here.'

Dina met her Dutch husband, who is a professional musician, at a concert in Brazil, by coincidence just before she came to Holland. But he was just going off for a year in Italy, so their relationship developed slowly and long-distance at first. After 5 years Dina graduated and decided to commit herself to her husband and to Holland. They married – rather than simply deciding to live together – partly because, as she says, 'I wanted our relationship to be stable and secure. I've known women who have lived with their boyfriends here and then the relationship has broken up. It is the woman who suffers especially and she may even have to leave the country.'

After Dina graduated from the Rotterdam Conservatorium she enrolled at Utrecht University for a further degree and plans to go on to do a doctorate there. In order to bring in an income – and because she enjoys it – Dina teaches music to individual students 5 days a week. She has also started up two international children's orchestras in The Hague, which she conducts to a high standard, and she performs regularly in a small renaissance music group. All this and pregnant with her first child!

Dina's advice for women who come to Holland to settle, particularly within the Dutch community, is simple. 'Learn good Dutch. You're always going to be a foreigner, but it will be appreciated. And you will enjoy a lot of things more – I can join in and understand jokes, for example.' Dina has not found any problems within her marriage in having two very different cultures, but she did find it difficult to feel accepted by her new

Dutch family. 'If you try to adapt too hard you lose your own identity. Draw the line very clearly for yourself and your culture. You are a foreigner and you stay a foreigner, but the nice thing is that you have the privilege of choosing what you want to take from Dutch culture. I have become more assertive since coming here, for example.'

Dina has a dream of going back to Brazil to live with her husband when they are older, to relax and enjoy life near the beach. But for now Holland is, she feels, a much better working environment for musicians, and they both love their work.

Be informed

There is a lot of information out there on settling in. Relocation has become big business in recent years, in recognition of the fact that moving to another country can bring all sorts of problems (see **Rosalind**'s story). You may have had the help of a relocation company when you moved here, to give practical support and advice on housing, education, etc. The best of these will hold your hand through all of the difficulties of settling in to a new country and provide you with detailed and accurate information on anything you wish to know about. We will draw a veil over the worst of them and hope you never have to suffer at their hands.

The Media

There are several excellent books of practical advice on settling in to an expat life in the Netherlands. (*Here's Holland* by Sheila Gazaleh-Weevers; *The Holland Handbook* by XPat Media; *Inside Information* by Caroline Gelderman; *Live and Work in Belgium, The Netherlands and Luxembourg* by André de Vries; *At Home in Holland* published by The American Women's Club; *The Simple Guide to Holland: Customs and Etiquette* by Mark T. Hooker; *The Low Sky* and *The Low Sky in Pictures* by Han van der Horst; *The Netherlands. A Practical Guide for the Foreigner and a Mirror for the Dutch* published by Prometheus/NRC Handelsblad). Read them all if you can. Magazines include The XPat Journal, Expats

Magazine, Roundabout, the ACCESS Newsletter, and the newsletters and magazines of the many expat clubs and societies. ACCESS offers a welcome package of publications for expats at 70 euros per pack.

On the more general side of being an expat, the excellent *Woman Abroad* magazine & website (www.womanabroad.com) addresses all kinds of issues which arise from expat life. Books to read include three by Robin Pascoe: *Living and Working Abroad: A Wives' Guide; Living and Working Abroad: A Parent's Guide;* and *Homeward Bound: A Spouse's Guide to Repatriation*. Robin has her own website at www.expatexpert.com. For parents there is also *Third Culture Kids* by David Pollack and Ruth van Reken and for students, *Culture Shock: A Student's Guide* by Robert Barlas and Guek-Cheng Pang.

In addition, a growing number of websites are geared to the needs of expats (e.g www.expatica.com; www.expatexchange.com; www.expataccess.com; www.elynx.nl; www.mumsabroad.com; www.xpat.nl; www.outpostexpat.nl; www.expatsonline.nl; www.britain.nl) and the beauty of those which offer a chatroom or message board service is that you can directly ask questions of other expats in Holland, before or after you arrive, and discuss issues of interest and concern.

Give it time

Nearly all of the women interviewed have stressed that things do get better after a rough patch. Many people have a honeymoon period to start off with, often followed by a bad time when the freshness and excitement start to wear off and you realise that Holland is not simply a pretty little country of windmills and canals and quaint gabled houses, but also has its problems and downside, just like everywhere else. The 'wall' tends to hit you after about six months, but it can be demolished at a swipe with determination or patiently dismantled bit by bit.

Ruth Prawar Jhabvala is an internationally renowned novelist and an expat herself, in India. In the introduction to one of her books of short stories

(*How I Became a Holy Mother and Other Stories*) she describes the cycle of stages that Europeans in India pass through: firstly, tremendous enthusiasm, everything Indian is marvellous; secondly, everything Indian not so marvellous; thirdly, everything Indian abominable. For some people, it ends there, for others the cycle goes on. She claims to be able to tell, after a few moments' conversation, at what stage of the cycle other Europeans are at. This may not be India, but the three-stage cycle is illuminating, is it not?

Things could be worse

Talk to any woman who's been here for longer than, say, five years, and she will tell you that things were, indeed, much worse in the old days. Everything is relative. Without wishing to be too much of a Pollyanna, I must point out some things that have improved considerably for expats, e.g.:

1. Communication is easier – international phone calls are cheaper; mobile phones mean children and partners can keep in touch with you and vice versa; e-mail keeps you in touch with friends across the world, cheaply and instantly.

2. The Internet has revolutionised the accessibility of information. Now you can search for a job, book a trip to Germany, read up on this week's news headlines, order your groceries (or your mother's – a friend who lives in Voorschoten organises grocery deliveries for her elderly parents in California through an online service) or take part in a discussion about euthanasia in Holland, all online.

3. Shops and stores stock a very much greater variety of goods than previously; OK, if you come from a centre of consumerism like London or San Francisco or Munich you might find this hard to grasp, but, truly, most of what you need you'll be able to find, somewhere, in Holland.

4. Travel is much cheaper these days. Flying to the UK costs about half of what it used to and transatlantic and other flights are also cheaper in real terms.

5. There are more and more international expats living in Holland. Indeed, the population of Amsterdam is now approximately 50%

non-Dutch. So there are more and more services geared to the needs of expats – for example, international schools (although sheer pressure of numbers on these is squeezing the services they can offer) – and more understanding of those needs.

6. More Dutch people speak English and are used to communicating in English.

7. There is a lot more information on offer to expats (see pages 22-23)

8. There are more and more career and educational opportunities for women, in English **and** it is very much simpler for accompanying spouses to get a work permit.

9. There is a much greater variety of **types**. British expat society in Holland, for example, used to be dominated by middle-aged, conservative, upper-middle class Englishwomen from the Home Counties – or so it seemed to those of us not from that particular milieu. They still exist, of course, but are heavily outnumbered by women of all social classes, ages and political viewpoints. A Scottish friend who has since gone back to Scotland always maintained that it was much more difficult to adjust to the English culture in the international community than to Dutch culture!

Knowing what you want to do

For many women, coming to live in a new country is an ideal time for a bit of self re-appraisal. Having been forced to give up a job, career, lifestyle, friends, etc., it's hardly surprising that fundamental questions like *Who am I? Where am I going?* should occur to a new arrival. Again, give it time. And while you're taking that time, do some research into what's available. There are many self-help books available for those who feel like a career/life change.

Build Your Own Rainbow. A Handbook for Career and Life Management by Hopson & Scally is a particularly useful one, with lots of challenging, fun exercises. It would make a good project for a month or so, to help you answer fundamental questions like *What changes do I want?* and *How do I make them happen?*

What Color is Your Parachute?: A Practical Manual for Job-Hunters and Career Changers by Richard Nelson Bolles is the American equivalent. It is immensely popular, selling 20,000 copies a month and translated into 10 languages. You can consult this book, along with others, in the small but quite comprehensive careers library at ACCESS in Plein, The Hague.

If you're keen on personality tests, *Do What You Are* by Paul Tieger and Barbara Barron-Tieger is a simplified version of the famous Myers-Briggs personality test, with results interpreted in terms of career possibilities. You can even enroll for a free careers course with Paul Tieger online at Barnes and Noble's 'university' at www.b&n.com.

Amazon has a *Choosing a Career* list on its website, with many more books, such as *The Complete Idiot's Guide to Changing Careers* by William Charland. The website www.queendom.com offers over 100 online tests – personality, intelligence, etc. – with around 20 specifically geared to careers, e.g. the *Aspiration Test* and the *Success Likelihood Test*. These need to be taken with a pinch of salt, but they are fun to do and may give you some insight into your strengths and weaknesses. Chapter 8 gives you some ideas about the practical possibilities for training while in the Netherlands if you want to acquire a new qualification.

The quiz

At the very least, before you start looking for something to do to fill your days, you should be able to answer this question in terms of priorities:

What do you want out of your daily activity (be it paid work or something else)?
Is it:
- Career development
- The knowledge that you are helping others
- The satisfaction of passing on skills or information
- Money

- The chance to be creative
- Doing something useful
- Relaxation
- Pleasure
- Social contacts
- Expanding your knowledge
- Passing the time, keeping boredom at bay
- Status

Put the list in order of priority from 1 – 12 (be honest) and think about your choices in terms of your list. If you have 'the chance to be creative' at the top, finance and accounting are probably not for you. If socialising is high on your list, don't set up an e-business or start freelance proofreading. If money or status are top of your list, it may be irrelevant where the other items lie. Make sure that there is at least a rough match between the priorities you have checked and what you do each day; if not, perhaps it's time for a change?

Finally, your fears

What's your fear?

Not being happy? All of the women in this book have spoken positively about life in Holland. I have not censored great swathes of material about what a rotten place this is and how much they all hate it, truly. Yes, quite a number have been unhappy at some time during their stay, but it was at least transient. Things do get better, life does change.

Not finding books / films / television in English? – no problem. See chapter 8.

Having no friends, being lonely – see chapter 9.

Having no job / leaving a good job – see chapters 1, 2 & 3.

The children not settling – see chapter 7.

For some fears, such as leaving elderly relatives behind, there are no easy answers. Some things will cause heartache, but most women are pretty good at coping and recovering when the chips are down. Life is also for living – look forward, try to do what you can now to make life good for yourself and your family. There is no point in looking back at what you might have had and feeling sorry for yourself. Look at the **Top ten tips** and the women's advice in chapter 10, look at the experiences of other women and the problems which they have overcome, and take heart.

PAID WORK

1   The job search

Kate's story

Kate, from England, is on her second time round in Holland. 'You're never sure if going back is the right thing, but I love it. I love being in Holland. We missed Europe when we were in the States, although we were with very warm, friendly people and there were brilliant opportunities for the children. But the more you move around, the more you know what you want from life.'

She came from Atlanta in the USA at the beginning of 2001, on account of her husband's job. The family had been in the USA for 3½ years, and before that in England. Last time round in Holland Kate hadn't worked, since her children were young. 'I had a big social life, doing coffee mornings and lunches and helping with the PTA. We had lots of visitors, and we went away a lot ourselves. Oh, and I had another baby. It was a nice period.'

This time in Holland was different. The children were older and all in school. Kate had passed the *Luba Uitzendbureau* (employment agency) sign every day on her way to and from the children's school in Oegstgeest for several weeks before she went in, almost on impulse, one day. There were no adverts to suggest that Luba deals with international staff, and Kate did not have a cv with her, but, she says, 'I was extremely excited to see what was out there. I hadn't been able to work in the States because of the green card situation, so when we got here I just jumped in with both feet. I went in and said, 'I'm a registered nurse. I know some Dutch and I'm learning more'.

The lady was very helpful. She wrote out a cv for me on the spot and sent it to a major international medical company near our house. But there were no opportunities available in nursing. After two weeks I got impatient and went back and said, 'I'll do something even if it's not nursing'. I had been thinking that perhaps I should move out of nursing anyway, and I was so lucky that a job had just become vacant for an administrator with a nursing background. I'm being trained to be an audit officer, using a medical database. I never thought of going down that path before, but I'm really enjoying it. My aim is to prove myself indispensable, as I'm on a temporary contract! My Dutch colleagues are extremely nice and helpful and we all get on well together. It's a good working environment. Of course, getting a job so quickly has meant that I didn't get a chance to do all those things I planned to do when I had a bit of time – but so what? I can stay up until midnight if I have to, to get things done.'

Kate still works hard at Dutch classes, and completes her homework assignments conscientiously – with help from her colleagues. For recreation, she sings in the British Choir, which she loves. 'All I have to take with me is my voice. No homework! It's wonderful.'

Kate describes her success in getting a good job as a sequence of lucky events, but it also has a lot to do with her determination, enthusiasm and positive attitude. She started off with an action plan, with contingency plans for doing TEFL work or helping out at the children's school if she couldn't get a job. But she was prepared to do almost anything – even enquiring about a job serving behind the counter in the local delicatessen – and she was also keen to work hard at improving her Dutch, which was very positively in her favour at the job interview. Her advice to other women coming to Holland? 'I'd strongly urge them to learn Dutch, to feel part of the community. Keep persevering. There are some lovely Dutch people out there – their attitude towards life is so good.'

Robin's story

Robin came to Amsterdam from the USA with her husband, because they wanted to have a new adventure and live in Europe. First, they tried life on a Greek island, but decided they are not really island people. On the island, though, they met two Dutch people who spoke so positively about Amsterdam that Robin and her husband read up some more about the city – they had never been there before – and in May 1999 they decided to pack up, get on a train and go and live there! 'We fell in love with Amsterdam immediately and found an apartment within a week. I love the cafés and restaurants, and the flowers. And people burn candles here.'

Robin and her husband decided to open up a candle shop, making their own candles in a workshop on the premises. Originally, they had planned to get a job, but when they went to an *uitzendbureau* (employment agency), they were surprised to find that – although there were plenty of suitable job vacancies – a work permit was not possible. So they had to open a business in order to stay in Holland. 'It was pretty easy, as far as setting up was concerned. The Dutch government is helpful to incomers setting up a business and we had a good immigration lawyer.'

The shop has since evolved and changed premises to the delightful Nieuwe Spiegelstraat 11B. Robin no longer makes her own candles, but buys in stock – sometimes using the Internet – and has branched out into soaps, bath salts and other exclusive perfumed toiletries. 80% of their customers are tourists, often American, and Robin enjoys meeting them.

However, Robin misses being part of a larger workplace and the opportunities for friendships which that brings. 'I'm pretty much alone in the shop and there's a lot of 'down' time between customers. In the US I made my best friends through work, but I haven't had that opportunity here and I don't have a best girlfriend. There is a lot to be said for knowing oneself as reflected in others, and I miss that. I look longingly at jobs at times – but I can't work without a permit. When I came here, I was interested in finding about myself, minus the support systems I had at home. Two years on, I'm still finding out.'

Robin's advice to women thinking about a move here is to talk to people first. 'I would have liked to have known more before we came. I would say, seek out women who are already there, through the Internet. And I wish I had had the Holland Handbook! You can't really know what it's going to mean to you, but if you have the chance, talk to people.'

How much do you *really* want a job?

Do you need to be in paid employment because of the money? If you have come to the Netherlands with a partner, it may be that his expat salary will comfortably cover your living expenses for a while. If so, ask yourself if you might be just as happy doing voluntary work, or gaining some additional qualifications, or pursuing an interest such as music or art, or simply taking stock for a while. However, you may feel that you need the kind of independence that even a small income can give you. Or perhaps you depend on your own income. In the latter two cases, it's obviously very important that you know the job market well.

The following quiz will help you to decide how much you really want paid employment:

1. **How much do you need an income from a job?**
a. Without it, I/we wouldn't be able to survive here
b. Without it, I/we would have a struggle to reach an acceptable standard of living
c. It would be nice to have some extra money, but to be honest, we don't really need it

2. **How much effort are you prepared to put into finding a paid job?**
a. I'd leave no stone unturned to find one
b. I'm prepared to take jobhunting very seriously, but it has to fit into the time I have available
c. I'll keep my ears open, and if I hear of anything really suitable, I'll look into it

3. **What compromises are you prepared to make in order to get a job?**
a. I'd do anything – move home if necessary, take on something I'm not keen on, work unsocial hours
b. I'd look carefully at any drawbacks and weigh them up against the benefits before deciding. The benefits would have to outweigh the drawbacks
c. The job would have to be really ideal before I'd make any changes in my circumstances

4. **How many hours a week do you want to work?**
a. Full-time
b. Full-time if necessary, but some time to myself during the week would be ideal
c. It must be part-time or not at all

5. **How much risk (e.g. of insecurity or failure) are you willing to take on with a new job?**
a. Not much. Security is the important thing to me
b. I don't mind taking a risk, but only if the job is really interesting
c. Risk wouldn't matter at all to me. I don't mind, if it's something interesting – I've nothing to lose

Mainly **A**s? You need to get to know the job market intimately and quickly. Follow the advice on finding a job in the rest of this chapter and in The Holland Handbook and The ACCESS Job Booklet.
Bs? You can afford to be pickier, but it's still important to keep looking.
Cs? You might also consider whether you'd be just as happy doing voluntary activities or taking some courses.

Rosemary was relocated to Holland in 1997 from the USA by her Computer Software company, as the general manager of the Benelux branch. 'I liked the entrepreneurial aspect but became disenchanted with the industry,' she says. When she was downsized by the company after a takeover and merger, at first Rosemary busied herself looking for another, similar job. She had 20 interviews in the first month and two job offers. But she turned both down – partly because they would have meant lengthy commuting at the beginning and end of each working day and therefore a lot less time to spend with her husband and daughter, but partly because 'I needed to evaluate what I'd done in order to be true to myself in going forward'. Rosemary gradually came to the decision that she no longer – after nearly 30 years of management experience – wanted to work in the business world. She wanted, instead, to do something of use and value to the community. She is still making plans to get involved in education and looking forward to a new kind of working life in the future.

Looking for a job

So, how do you go about looking for a paid job in the Netherlands? You need to have several strings to your bow, as with any important and complex task, but a sensible starting point would be the Internet, to give you an idea of what's available.

Job-searching on the web

Below I give a list of URLS (website addresses) of organisations that can help you in your search, but, of course, they do tend to date very quickly.

These websites are geared to the English-speaking jobseeker; they are in English and the jobs on offer are for English speakers (although many require a second European language and some prefer a working knowledge of Dutch, in addition to fluent English).

www.englishlanguagejobs.nl
www.adamsrecruit.nl
www.kellyservices.nl
www.undutchables.nl
www.uniquemls.com
www.bluelynx.nl
www.dacumac.nl
www.expatica.com

www.jobserve.com (international site for IT jobs – there are always some in the Holland section)

www.newscientistjobs.com (nearly all professional scientific and engineering jobs in Europe which require English as a working language are advertised in New Scientist; type in Netherlands as your keyword and you will find plenty of vacancies)

'Despite the fact that I've been out of the workforce for four years, I realise that I have a lot to offer this organisation. It is also evident that they respect all of my experience and not just that which was salaried. I can't believe I'm 38 and I've finally found my niche.'

The websites below are all in Dutch, but all have jobs for English speakers, also. The best way to locate these is to key in 'English' as your *trefwoord* (keyword) when starting a search. This will usually bring up all job vacancies which specify English as the language of the workplace.

www.jobnews.nl
www.monsterboard.nl
www.adecco.nl
www.stepstone.nl

The irritating thing about many job-search websites is that you are forced to choose from various categories – administrative, financial, managerial – when searching. The better ones will allow you to search all categories at one go, if you narrow down your other terms (geographical area, etc.) and specify 'English' in the keyword space.

Using an *uitzendbureau*

Celine, from Canada, found a job in her field of medical communications through an *uitzendbureau*. 'I'd been out of the workplace for four years and my initial application was for a position for which I was overqualified. I was just hoping to get my foot in the door after having been home with my children for four years. I think a lot of women who come here settle for jobs that they're overqualified for, just to get out into the workplace. When I didn't get a response after two weeks, I assumed that it was because I was too old or too long out of work. But, in fact, the company was scrambling to create a suitable position for me and were thrilled to have someone with my experience. Despite the fact that I've been out of the workforce for four years, I realise that I have a lot to offer this organisation. It is also evident that they respect all of my experience and not just that which was salaried. I can't believe I'm 38 and I've finally found my niche.'

A number of job search sites on the Internet are the websites of office-based *uitzendbureaus*, or job placement agencies. You can register your cv, or resume, with any number of *uitzendbureaus*. Some are geared specifically to the English-speaking market and some cater both for Dutch speakers and those who wish to work in English. They do not charge you for doing this, nor for finding you a job (they make their money by levying charges on the companies who register vacancies with them), so you can sign up for as many as you like. None will take you on willingly without a work permit in place, though.

All of the major *uitzend* companies have websites and most allow you to register online. Some let you add your cv as an attachment, which means that you have control over your own design and layout, whereas others have an online form which you must fill in. This can cramp your style considerably. In fact, the whole business of sending off a general cv to an agency can be very constraining and perhaps even reduce your chances of finding out about all of the interesting possibilities out there. There may well be jobs which you could do, but don't match the profile on your general cv, or don't match the search category (administrative, technical, etc.) which you've been registered under. It may be best, if you have the time, to make a visit in person to speak to a job consultant in several *uitzendbureaus*, before sending off your cv. That way you can make a personal impression first, and talk about your qualifications and experience without having them pre-judged from your cv.

Networking

Knowing people is vitally important for women who set up a business or work freelance. Personal contact is the main way to build up a client base, and that's something you have to work at constantly. But it's also important in getting a job.

Norma (see her story in chapter 10) has worked as a freelance English teacher for several years for many different organisations and institutions. 'I've never once been for an interview for a job,' she says. 'It's all come through networking.'

Ella decided that she ought to try to get back into the workplace after several years here. She had been a university lecturer in South Africa, but in Afrikaans, so she couldn't easily break into the academic world in Holland. She found that the *uitzendbureaus* she tried were not helpful in finding her suitable work, but that networking was for her the best way. She had been Chairlady of the South African Women's Club and very involved in community organisations. When the post of administrative manager at the South Africa Chamber of Commerce came up, she was able to persuade them that her skills fitted the job profile best. Her advice is to get involved in organisations such as the International Women's Contact so that people get to know you and what you can offer.

Newspaper advertisements

This is the traditional way to search for a job, but your task can be expensive – buying several papers each week and a lot of frustration and wasted time searching through hundreds of unsuitable vacancies which are only available to those with good Dutch language skills. The Internet has largely supplanted newspaper adverts as the best way of looking for a job, but if you want to try anyway, buy the Saturday editions of *De Telegraaf*, *Algemeen Dagblad* and your regional daily newspaper.

The cv or resume

There are lots of books – and Internet articles – on how to write the perfect cv, e.g. *The Perfect cv* by Tom and Ella Jackson. You can do a search on Amazon and find many more. *Uitzendbureaus* will also help you to put together a suitable cv for the job market here. The gist of their advice is always the same – make it look smart and professional, make sure it contains no mistakes and keep it businesslike and to the point. As if you would neglect any of these! Microsoft Word has several attractive templates for cv writing and a 'resume wizard' whereby you can customise your own. Whatever you choose, do get someone to cast a dispassionate eye over it for you, before sending it off.

'Being young and female can be a disadvantage. But I met people who saw I'd more potential and sent me to a different sector, where the work is much more interesting. Things have gone well since then.'

If, like many women over 30, you have had a number of career changes (and perhaps a break to bring up children or follow your husband around) you need to view your cv as something fluid and be prepared to tailor your document to the specific vacancies which you are interested in. On a general cv, you might decide to leave out details such as the summer job you once had as an assistant conference organiser long ago when you were a student – but then you might see a post advertised for a conference organiser. You can re-vamp your cv to include, in a high-profile kind of a way, that summer job. Be prepared for several re-vampings if you are applying for a number of jobs. And always tailor your covering letter very carefully to the specific job you're applying for. With virtually universal access to word processing facilities nowadays, there is no excuse for sending off the same vague and general stuff to everyone.

You can send off unsolicited cv s or post a general cv on many job-search websites for free and see what responses that brings. I've never met anyone who has had any luck with the latter approach, but that doesn't mean it won't work for you. Anything is worth a try if you're keen. And good things can develop from unpromising beginnings.

Rachel is English, but lived in Holland for most of her childhood, with a 5-year stint in Chicago in the middle years. She recently returned to Holland, where her parents still live, after a year in Italy in a poorly paid job teaching English. Rachel started off by sending her cv round a number of companies, but was disheartened to get no replies, although she has a degree from a top UK university. She eventually found a job in an oil company, through an *uitzendbureau*, but it took a while for her to find her niche there. At first she found herself in a section where, as she puts it, 'Being young and female can be a disadvantage. But I met people who saw I'd more potential and sent me to a different sector, where the work is much more interesting. Things have gone well since then.'

However, Rachel finds that being young and female is generally easier – and safer – here than in either Italy or England. 'There are no drunken yobs, like in England. And there are no problems going into a bar on my own here, unlike in Italy. I can travel easily anywhere.'

Advertise yourself on your own website

Better than posting your cv on other people's websites, is to set up your own website (see chapter 3, page 65 for advice on how to do it). Once you have your cv online, with link pages giving details of projects you have worked on, perhaps your views on what makes a good manager/editor/IT trainer and any other relevant stuff (don't overdo it, though), then make a list of potential employers in your field. Send e-mails to the HR managers with a short but interesting message indicating that you're looking for new opportunities and providing a hyperlink to your website. Make sure that your website has a link to your e-mail address, and sit back and wait for the replies! With luck, you will have at least a few interested responses and hopefully even interviews and job offers.

N.B. It's worth remembering the 3 Ts of working – temperament, talent and training. If you have all of them in good measure for the job you want, then you're almost all the way there. If one or more is missing, think again.

2 Working for an organisation

Florence's story

Her Excellency Judge Florence Mumba from Zambia is one of only two women judges at the International War Crimes Tribunal in The Hague and currently vice-president of the court. The majority are men who are considerably older than her (she is 52). You may remember seeing her on television when she delivered her verdict – dignified and moving – on the first Serbian rapists to be convicted by the Tribunal. Florence came to the Netherlands in 1997 when she was elected by the United Nations to serve as a judge at the Tribunal; it was her first time living outside Zambia and she found life very, very different here.

'The weather is very difficult to get used to. It's so hostile, you have to hibernate in winter. I suffered during my first year, but now I am more used to it.' She laughs a lot – an infectious laugh, almost a giggle. It seems incongruous that a woman whose professional life is spent dealing with the most appalling atrocities should be so jolly and cheerful in conversation. There is absolutely no pomposity about her, no sense of inflated self-importance.

When Florence first came, she had two school-aged children with her. 'The other judges – the men – wondered how I would manage. Well, my children were older and they had to share the household duties. I wasn't used to having no home help – in Zambia, the maid came at 6 in the morning and now I had to learn to get up in time to make my own breakfast! And the shopping was difficult at first, having to eat Dutch food – but then I discovered the market in the Hobbemaplein*, where you can buy all sorts of vegetables we have in my country, and dried fish, which we eat a lot at home.'

She tries not to take work home with her, but rather stays at the office later if necessary. Saturdays are for being at home and relaxing. Sundays involve churchgoing and holidays give the opportunity to explore Europe a little.

'I'm fortunate that I haven't been ill. It's a stressful job, so I take care of my health. I walk a lot – there are lovely parks in The Hague – and I've done some aerobics now and again.'

Florence's two younger children came with her to Holland; the two older ones decided after 18 months to join the family in Europe, too. One studies in Eire, the other has learned Dutch well enough to be accepted onto a course at a Dutch college (yes, it can be done) and now studies engineering. Her husband was already retired when they came and looked on the stay as a something of a holiday; however, when boredom started to set in, he found himself a job, too, in a completely different area to his wife's. So the family members have all adjusted in their own ways to a very different lifestyle here – which is just as well, since Judge Mumba had the honour to be elected to serve a second 4-year term of office at the Court from autumn 2001.

Hettie's story

Hettie came to Holland at the end of 1999 from New Zealand, where she was principal of a high school, in response to an advertisement for a headmaster (for complex reasons, her title is Headmaster) for the International School in Hilversum. 'My husband had just retired and for most of my life I had followed him around, so now we switched.'

* see chapter 9, page 137

They had been thinking of returning to Europe now that their two boys had left home, so Hettie's husband became a trailing spouse ('He would hate to be called that!'). He travels a lot throughout Europe and has time to develop his hobbies, so is relaxed and comfortable with living here.

Hettie is passionate about the International Baccalaureate (IB) programme.* Both of her sons went through the programme and she found being an IB parent very exciting. She was attracted to the school in Hilversum because of its high reputation and the fact that it had been very successfully involved in bi-lingual education. 'Most Dutch people don't know that Holland has been in the vanguard of bi-lingual education in the middle years IB programme, but word has filtered out to the world network.'

Hettie also likes the size of the school – small enough so that she is able to see every student on his or her birthday – and the fact that she is still able to teach classes, rather than be tied to administrative work all day. This year she is regularly tracking individual student classes for a day – even down to using the student toilets – in order to find out what it is like to be a student in her school.

After two years in post, Hettie feels she is getting into her stride. The first year brought the major challenge of moving school building, into a newly renovated Dutch Modernist building. At the same time, she was making contacts in the school and local community and establishing networks across Europe. Having overseen the setting up a school website, Hettie now wants to establish a good intranet structure for staff and students.

As anyone who has ever worked in a school will know, being a head teacher is an immensely challenging job, with long working hours. But Hettie has an excellent support in her husband and they build in mini-break honeymoon treats for themselves every so often.

* This is a curriculum which leads to an internationally recognised pre-university diploma. It is taught in many schools throughout the world.

Hettie's advice? 'Write out a daily schedule which balances everything out – work, leisure, Dutch – and stick to it. But I'm my own worst enemy!

If work takes over my world I don't do much to stop it. But don't underestimate the impact your career is going to have on your life and everyone in the family.'

Holland is the eighth country Hettie and her husband have lived in. 'After Papua New Guinea, Europe looks very normal! I think you should give learning the language of a country first priority, and I am sorry I have not done that, because it gives you access to the culture. But just because you share a language with someone, it doesn't mean you share their culture. The comfortable culture for me doesn't exist in a geographical place – it's about tolerance, the sharing of differences, excitement. That's my home, in an international setting.'

Organisations which employ international staff

The inter-governmental organisations

There are at least 11 inter-governmental international organisations with offices in the Netherlands, where English is the working language (or one of the working languages). These are:

CFC	Common Fund for Commodities, Amsterdam
CTA	Technical Centre for Agriculture and Rural Cooperation, Wageningen
EPO	European Patent Office, The Hague
Europol	European Police Office, The Hague
ICJ	International Court of Justice, The Hague
ICTY	International Criminal Tribunal for the Former Yugoslavia, The Hague
ISNAR	International Service for National Agricultural Research, The Hague
NATO	Consultation, Command and Control Agency, The Hague

OPCW   Organisation for the Prohibition of Chemical Weapons,
            The Hague
UNU-INTEC   The United Nations University: Institute for New
            Technologies, Maastricht

Each has its own website, but the Permanent Mission of Italy to International Organisations in Geneva acts as a gatekeeper for vacancies on the Internet. If you go to http://missions.itu.int/~italy/vacancies you will find links to the vacancy pages of all of the above organisations. One other organisation not on the above list is ESA, the European Space Agency, at www.esa.int. It has a job vacancies page on its site.

Some of these organisations are better than others for jobseekers. EPO, ESA and OPCW tend to have the most vacancies, some being specialist posts for scientists, but there are also some general administrative jobs. You have to be a citizen of certain countries for most of these organisations, and often you must be able to speak an additional European language. Conditions and salaries tend to be good compared to the Dutch job market, especially at the higher professional levels.

The international schools

There are about 30 international schools in Holland. ACCESS keeps a list, and there are lists on many expat websites or you can go to www.sio.nl. Stichting Internationaal Onderwijs (SIO) is an organisation which provides detailed information on international schools in Holland and its website has links to all of their websites. The biggest are The American School of The Hague (ASH, located in Wassenaar), The British School in the Netherlands (BSN, located in The Hague, Voorschoten and Assen) and The International School of Amsterdam (ISA, located in Amstelveen). All take children from kindergarten or junior age up to age 18 or 19. ASH and BSN post job vacancies on their websites. They employ not only teachers (both permanent and substitute, or supply), but also administrators, secretaries, librarians, nurses, IT personnel and others. However, there is a warning on the ASH site: 'Due to the high volume of resumes submitted each week it may take up to 6 weeks to process each one.'

In addition to the schools, there are many English-speaking playgroups, nurseries and kindergartens which cater for the international market. ACCESS has a list and it may be worth contacting a few if you have a qualification to work with young children.

'I found a niche which I really love and I'm still happy with it. I keep the public happy. The advent of the web and e-mail has made a huge difference, and the nature of my job has changed enormously. But a lot of it is down to what you make of it. I love it.'

The Open University

In chapter 5, I extol the virtues of the Open University as a place where you can gain new qualifications and expand your horizons. It is also an employer of quite a number of expats, as associate lecturers. If you have a postgraduate degree in a subject – or experience in the business world – you could check the website at www.open.ac.uk to see if there are vacancies. The annual closing date for applications is normally around mid-July, for courses that start in February. The work involves distance tuition – i.e. being available at the end of the telephone or e-mail address – and grading regular student assignments.

The Embassies

It may be worth getting in touch with your country's embassy to see whether they employ local staff. Many do. The British Embassy employs over 60 staff, of whom about half are locally employed. Posts do become available fairly regularly, as people come and go quite frequently, and are advertised in the newspapers and on the website (which is worth a visit even if you are not looking for a job – www.britain.nl). The Embassy will also accept unsolicited cvs (unlike some of the inter-governmental organisations) and these should be addressed to the Management Officer.

Jan is Information Librarian at the British Embassy. Eleven years ago, when she was busy editing the British Women's Club magazine, a friend told her about 'the perfect job' at the Embassy. She sent in her cv, went for interview and was offered the job. 'I found a niche which I really love and I'm still happy with it.' Jan works for the Press and Public Affairs Section, giving the public information on all aspects of both life in the UK and expat life in Holland. 'I keep the public happy. The advent of the web and e-mail has made a huge difference, and the nature of my job has changed enormously. But a lot of it is down to what you make of it. I love it.'

Shell

In the old days, Shell was the major employer of British expats in Holland. 'Shell wives' seemed to comprise the majority of women at the British Women's Club, and they were wives first and foremost, with no jobs of their own. By 1995, things had begun to change and women were no longer all content to follow their husbands willy-nilly across the world while sacrificing their own careers. In that year, in response to a clear need, the Spouse Employment Centre was set up by Kathleen van der Wilk-Carlton to give advice and information to partners who want to pursue their own careers. If your partner works for Shell, you have probably been contacted by the Centre and offered help if you wish it. Partners have access to lists of job vacancies in Shell and are given information on general job prospects in Holland and volunteering and educational opportunities.

Shell is still a big employer of expats. If you do not have a Shell partner, but still fancy working for the organisation, go to www.shell.com/careers-en to see what vacancies are available.

Other companies

Again, ACCESS has a list of the major British and American companies in Holland. Almost without exception, they have a website with a job vacancies section – for example www.elsevier.nl. If the site is in Dutch, the word to look for is *vacatures*. You can simply pick a company you fancy working for, and check out their vacancies through their website. Keep checking regularly, too, as situations can change rapidly. A couple of ISP (Internet Service Provider) companies that offer jobs from time to time are Chello Broadband (http://info.nld.chello.nl), which actively solicits CVs in English, and Ripe Network Coordination Centre (www.ripe.net).

However, if you are vaguely looking around for some job or other in business or industry, your search will probably be more efficiently and effectively conducted if you go through a job agency, or *uitzendbureau*. The very best thing to do is employ both strategies – your own Internet searches, using both company sites and job-search sites, as well as signing on with one or more agencies. And, if you can, set up your own website to advertise yourself (see chapters 1 and 3).

Nineteen of the women in this book – 38% – work for a large organisation. Most, I think, enjoy their jobs and would recommend their workplace to others. Of those 19, only three work part-time, although a couple started part-time and became full-time as their jobs grew. Ten have children still at home, six of them with primary-aged children (or younger).

3　Freelancing and business

Donna's story

Donna, who is originally a research specialist in haematology, has lived outside her home country (the USA) for 31 years, across 6 different continents – 'all for oil,' as she says. Her husband is a petroleum engineer, and still travels around the world, living away from home for long periods. But Donna has stayed put in Holland since 1978. When she first came here she worked as a trainer for the USA Girl Scouts and as an American Red Cross trainer. She was also on the board of the American Women's Club and organised travel trips for the members – including leading one to China in 1982. That year a change in family circumstances – her husband lost his job – meant that Donna had to find work herself. First, she tried going back to the USA and taking a job in business. But it wasn't right for her. 'If you stay out of your home country too many years you're a misfit.' So Donna came back to Holland and set up a business she called Helping Hands. This was an au pair, catering and cleaning agency, supplying services to international expats.

'There's always someone willing to pay for something they don't want to do themselves. You find a niche in the market and you go for it. You have to start slowly and small, and be flexible. Flexibility is very important in the international market.'

Helping Hands was very successful for 10 years and enabled Donna to be financially independent. During this time she and her husband adopted their son from overseas. 'If you are a citizen of one country, resident in another and adopt from a third country, life gets very complicated. It took us seven years to sort out the paperwork.'

By 1992 Donna had become aware of another gap in the market and planned to move on to a new challenge. Through Helping Hands she constantly found people who were desperately looking for an international pre-school facility. She started to look around for premises. 'It took a year to find the right building (in Wassenaar) and seven years to get permission from the local council to change the use of the building.' So Donna simply opened up The Activity Shop without permission and dared them to close it down. They didn't, but as Donna says, it took a lot of lawyers' fees to stop them. She felt herself to be bucking against a male-dominated bureaucracy. 'If we'd taken no for an answer we wouldn't be here.'

The Activity Shop now has a staff of 12 and 110 students (mostly part-time). It offers four pre-school classes and after-school activities and summer camps for older children, to the international community. It functions as a sort of mini-school, and is heavily oversubscribed. Sharon's daughter, Marissa, was very happy there. 'Donna is very organised and surrounds herself with knowledgeable staff. The children go on lots of outings – it seemed that wherever we went as a family, Marissa had already been there with the Activity Shop.'

Another string to Donna's bow is the registered charity which she runs, called Children to Children. It arose out of the Romanian crisis, when Donna organised – and even drove herself – truckloads of food, medical supplies and blankets across Europe in winter. She still collects good quality clothes, food and toys to pass on to the Sisters of Charity for distribution.

Donna has some hard-hitting advice for any woman planning to start up in business in Holland. 'Unless you have the constitution of an ox, you won't make it! Be determined, persistent and don't take no for an answer. Delegate – but to the right people. Choose someone with a calm personality, who is Dutch, to help you through the bureaucracy. (Donna has an office manager, Mariska, who deals with all the administrative details, and the two work very well together). Don't do your own accounting and tax. Find the line between being assertive and aggressive and go for it. And have a sense of humour!'

In case all that advice hasn't persuaded you that life as a businesswoman can be tough, you should know that Donna still works a 70-hour week in order to get everything done!

Natasha's story

Natasha is Russian. Like Julie, she came to live in Holland because she fell in love with a Dutchman. Natasha met her husband, Diederik, in 1994 when she was living with her son in Germany and giving Russian lessons. Diederik was one of her students. 'He found it easier to marry me than to continue with the Russian course!' In 1995 they married and Natasha came to live in Holland. She tried learning Dutch through a course at Leiden University, but didn't like the way they taught and ended up teaching herself (as a language teacher, it was a case of physician heal thyself) and is now comfortable speaking the language in public.

Natasha had her own language school in Moscow, offering Business English, Marketing and Public Relations, which she had built up from scratch to a thriving business with 150 students. Here in Holland, she is busy establishing a new language school. She was recently nominated by City of The Hague for a prize for the best start-up business. 'I didn't win the prize, but it's not important, because at the competition I made connections and got orders, so I didn't lose. I achieved publicity and that was my goal. Also, I'm not afraid to make presentations in Dutch any more, because I won over my fear when I had to make a public speech at the competition.'

When she first came to Holland, Natasha tried to apply for jobs in language schools. She found she was offered freelance work but never had the possibility of a permanent job. 'I said to myself, I'll do it myself. I can do it better and I should get the benefit. My husband and I worked it out together, the concept of a Virtual Language School, where we provide in-house language training for companies. We have special tests to check learning styles, so we can personalise our teaching. We are very flexible and will work weekends if people want. My credo is that good teachers should be paid well, and should be paid for their preparation time. Our prices are competitive and the students like our flexibility, so it's been a success so far.'

Natasha likes to make her contacts through networking and joined International House in Leiden and Connecting Women in order to meet other international women. Her advice to newcomers is to read and learn about the history and culture of the country. 'If you want to do business it's absolutely essential. If you want to succeed you have to show you know and respect the culture, then people will trust you. If you know a couple of idioms and use them, it's appreciated.'

Working freelance

If you can't find or don't want a regular paid job, perhaps you have a qualification or skill you could use to make some money or simply to make yourself useful to the community? Look through the following list – there's almost certainly at least one item here that you could take on.

Art

Can you paint, or teach art to others, including children? Do you know a craft – patchwork, pottery, dough dollies? **Jean** started to teach painting 15 years ago. Her first classes were run from home with two pupils. Now she runs a thriving art studio with 120 students (mainly international expat women), a shop and picture framing business, and has plans to expand. She does all of the teaching herself and in addition she continues to paint (at night, the only time available in her busy schedule!) lovely watercolours of buildings in The Hague. One of her paintings was presented to Kofi Annan and hangs in the UN building in New York and she has had commissions from the Dutch Government, embassies, inter-governmental organisations and private individuals. Jean has had no formal art training, so in theory her success is open to anyone willing to try, but as she says, 'You have to have a great deal of determination'. Like Donna, she also works hugely long hours each week. See her website at www.studiojean.nl.

'There are a lot of expat women with time – and money – on their hands. Beauty therapy is a luxury which they enjoy having. I'd say there are great possibilities for any kind of business which is aimed at the English-speaking market.'

If you prefer to produce tangible goods rather than teach, you could sell your products at craft fairs. The American Women's Club in The Hague holds two major craft fairs every year, at Easter and Christmas, (standards are very high) and most schools and local communities have smaller ones around Christmas. **Jan** (chapter 10) makes beautiful glass bowls and hanging panels, which she sells at craft fairs. **Judy** (chapter 7) has found an outlet in England, through a relative there, for her hand-painted plates and bowls.

Baking/cooking

A friend of mine used to do children's birthday cakes and grown-up party catering for the expat community; she had a good business going and since she's left I haven't heard of anyone else doing it in a serious way. **Luisa** (chapter 8) runs Italian cookery and language courses from her home.

Beauty

Claire opened up her own beauty salon when she was only 20. She trained in England and came to Holland, where her parents live and where she went to school, when she was 18. Initially, she worked in a beauty salon in Wassenaar for two years and then rented her own premises with another woman, to keep costs down. 'There was a lot of paperwork involved and I found it difficult, but my parents and my husband kept encouraging me. My husband, who's Dutch, helped with the bureaucracy. I advertised in publications for the international community and found that I needed very little advertising, as each advert brought in so many clients and I could only take a maximum of about 50 a month anyway, working on my own. For the past six years I haven't advertised at all, and my clientele has shifted mainly to the Dutch market, with business coming by word of mouth.'

Claire didn't speak Dutch when she first worked in Holland, but she found it quite easy to pick up the language in the salon where her colleagues were speaking Dutch all day. Beauty therapists in salons are not particularly well paid, but Claire found that working for herself she could make a nice living if she worked full-time, although she has two young children now and chooses not to. 'There are a lot of expat women with time – and money – on their hands. Beauty therapy is a luxury which they enjoy having. I'd say there are great possibilities for any kind of business which is aimed at the English-speaking market.'

Childcare

If you like children and have the patience and time to look after them, there are always mothers seeking part-time and full-time childcare. Look for small ads on school notice boards (or put up your own ad), in school newsletters, local papers and on expat Internet sites. If you want a full-time live-in job, look in the *Gouden Gids* (yellow pages) under au pair bureaus, or subscribe to the weekly English magazine, *The Lady*, which features pages and pages of adverts for nanny and au pair jobs. There are nearly always a few in Holland.

It also accepts adverts from would-be au pairs looking for work and you can submit your advert (and buy a 12-week subscription) through the website at www.lady.co.uk.

Could you help women seeking childcare work by setting up an agency to provide other women with nannies/carers for their children? **Donna**'s Helping Hands Agency was very successful in the expat community for 10 years, and was wound up only because she moved on to another venture. You could even follow in her footsteps and open an international pre-school facility – but remember, you need the constitution of an ox to succeed!

Coaching

Julia (chapter 9) heard a BBC radio programme about life coaching and decided to explore that avenue here in the Netherlands. She set up a freelance business as a coach in February 2000 and has found plenty of clients in both the expat and Dutch communities. Her website is at www.juliaferguson.com. A coach is a kind of mentor, who listens, helps you to define what you want and steers you towards achieving your goals. If you are interested in becoming a coach, two useful books are *Take Yourself to the Top: The Secrets of America's #1 Career Coach* by Laura Berman-Fortgang (UK edition also available) and *Co-active Coaching: New Skills for Coaching People Towards Success in Work and Life* by Laura Whitworth. The International Coach Federation has a comprehensive website at www.coachfederation.org. Julia is the contact person for the Dutch chapter. Another useful link is at www.coachville.com. You could also key in 'life coaching' to an Internet search engine and you will find plenty of training courses and sites run by individual coaches (you will also find sites offering coach tours of Iceland and details of baseball coaching federations, but that's the Internet for you).

However, 'counselling' (which can be a very slippery concept to define) on a professional basis is best left to those professionally trained and supervised. In my experience as a psychologist, people who turn to psychologists and counsellors are often those with very serious problems who are right at the end of their tether. Would you want to deal with potential suicides, anorexia, sexual abuse, violent relationships and all the desperate misery that goes along with these situations, without full training and regular supervision? Indeed, if you had a real need for help yourself, wouldn't you want to be able to rely on the professional experience of the person you consulted? If you are looking for a counsellor, ACCESS has a counselling section, where all counsellors are qualified at least to master's Degree level. If you want to explore an interest in counselling, there is a counselling course in English which runs in The Hague. See www.counselling.nl/cpcab.html. Also, the NEC (www.nec.ac.uk) and the College of Counselling (www.collegeofcounselling.com) offer various types of counselling courses, by correspondence. Both are UK-based non-profit institutions.

Computing

Julia*, from the USA, runs a freelance business offering individual computer support and problem-solving for women in their own homes. 'If I advertised aggressively I could work all day every day, there's such a demand in the international community. But with two little children I don't want to do that.'

Julia came to Holland for a 2 – 3 year stint because of her husband's job (she'll be gone by the time you read this, so there's no point in giving her contact number, I'm afraid). With her previous work experience at the computer giant, IBM, she was able to help solve a neighbour's computer problems. The neighbour referred another friend, who did some babysitting for Julia in exchange for technical help, and things just grew from there.

Website design is another area where there is a huge market for small-scale services. If you know how to set up a website, even at quite a basic level, you could advertise your services either as a teacher or a designer. If your charges are reasonable, you could find yourself very busy indeed.

* this is a different Julia from the Julia in the previous section on coaching!

Design

In chapter 8 are details of courses in garden design and interior design. If you gained a qualification in design, you could offer your services to the expat community and perhaps make a new career for yourself in that direction.

Entertaining

You could become very popular very quickly with a lot of people if you offer a party service for children. Clowns, magicians, balloon sculptors and general party organisers are always in demand. Lots of patience and lots of stamina required!

Housecleaning and ironing

These are reasonably well paid if you need some ready cash while you look around for/do other things.

Music

Can you teach piano or keyboard or recorder? There are many parents looking for private lessons for their children.

Selling franchised articles

The obvious item which everyone has heard of is Tupperware. I was once invited to an expat Tupperware party, and I believe they still exist. You can check the Tupperware website at www.tupperware.nl if you are interested. But there are other sales opportunities.

Liz started selling Usborne children's books in a small way five years ago, through book parties and school fairs, and has built up a thriving business. She came to Holland because of her husband's job in 1984, with a 6-month-old baby and a 3-year-old. 'For the first 10 years I was a Mum. Then my daughter went to boarding school and I wanted something for myself.

At that time my sister in England worked as a sales representative for Usborne children's books and she mentioned to me that they were planning to expand into Europe. I contacted them and started out by bringing one box of books over here in my car, to see if I could sell them.'

'We offer book fairs to international schools, nurseries and playgroups and I also do parties in people's houses. The more I do, the busier I get.'

Liz had to make an investment and buy those books – there was no sale or return for start-up businesses. 'I went very carefully at first, and it took a while to get accepted by the international schools, but now I have others working with me, in Eindhoven, Haarlem and Amsterdam, and I work in The Hague, together with a friend who represents other publishers. We offer book fairs to international schools, nurseries and playgroups and I also do parties in people's houses. The more I do, the busier I get. I think it's very worthwhile – I'd rather do books than Tupperware or jewellery. I enjoy the contact with children and, when I can, I give a little talk on how a book is made.'

Liz gets a lot of satisfaction from her work and really appreciates its flexibility. It fits round her family commitments and she can do as much or as little as she likes.

Sewing

When **Jean** came to Holland she wanted to make some money, so she set up a business designing and making clothes for expat women. It was very successful, but unfortunately she had to give up because problems with her hands meant that she could no longer sew. There may be a gap in the market there right now. 'Finishing' is a service you sometimes see advertised in craft magazines, for women (like me, I must admit), who like to start tapestries but never quite get round to completing them. I have a cupboard full of nearly-finished projects which I wish some good fairy would transform into cushions and pictures for me!

Teaching English as a Second Language

This can be a godsend as a portable career for the expat spouse. See **Norma**'s story (chapter 10). You would obviously want to be qualified before attempting to get work, and happily it is possible to gain a recognised qualification without leaving Holland. The British Language Teaching Centre in Amsterdam (020 - 622 36 34) offers both intensive and extensive courses in teaching English to adults, leading to the UK-recognised Cambridge/RSA certificate. And now the OCR (Oxford, Cambridge, RSA) examining board in England is offering online tuition for the same certificate, and also the more advanced diploma. You need to be videoed for the assessment of your teaching practice, and send the videotapes to your personal tutor in England. Their website is at www.olionline.com.

Another distance course is run by the Open University, called Teaching English to Speakers of Other Languages Worldwide. It is designed for those who already have some teaching experience – although not necessarily in teaching English – and preferably qualifications already. You have a tutor in the country in which you live, which must be an advantage.

If you are not confident that you could start a certificate course immediately, or you simply want a taster of what is involved in teaching English, the National Extension College (NEC) has a pre-certificate course called Introduction to TEFL, by correspondence.

Tutoring

With literally thousands of international students across the country studying for examinations, many of whom need extra help with some subjects, perhaps you could help here. You may be bilingual and able at least to give conversation practice in one language. **Lisa** (chapter 9) takes students for French lessons. Or you may have a teaching qualification and be able to teach certain subjects at examination level. I occasionally give extra tuition in Advanced Level Psychology, a subject I used to teach. It's rewarding, both in terms of personal satisfaction and, of course, financially.

Wine

Cristina is a South African wine connoisseur and educator with a passion for her subject. See her story in chapter 8. In South Africa she was employed in the wine industry. When she moved to England she set up wine appreciation courses, which were extremely popular and gave her great pleasure and satisfaction. Recently moved to the Netherlands, she is planning to explore similar opportunities in the expat community. Having attended one of her courses as guinea pig, I can thoroughly recommend them.

Writing

Is there a book inside you somewhere? Now could be your opportunity to get it written. With slick and simple word-processing available on every PC, and the Internet as your virtual reference library, much of the old pain and slog of writing has disappeared.

Sheila (chapter 4) wrote a book which has been popular with both tourists and expats for many years (*Here's Holland*). She saw a need, started very simply with a pamphlet, and ended up as a well-known author. Perhaps you could do the same?

An inspiring book for would-be authors is *Is There A Book Inside You?* By Dan Poynter and Mandy Bingham. This is more useful if the book inside you is non-fiction, although it does address fiction, too. For truly creative souls, *The Complete Idiot's Guide to Creative Writing* by Laurie Rozakis, is a guide to writing novels, short stories, plays, poetry and screenplays. The Open College of the Arts offers several creative writing courses by distance learning, and in addition there are many correspondence courses in writing. Chapter 5 has more information on how to find information on courses.

If you don't have a book in there, then at least you might have an article or two. You may not be a professional journalist, but it's easy to get into print if you're prepared to write on a volunteer basis. Every club, society, church group, school and institution has a newsletter or magazine and most are absolutely desperate for articles. Just write your piece and send it off to the editor. If you want a wider audience – worldwide, in fact – go on the web. Many websites solicit articles from their readers. *Tales From a Small Planet* (www.talesmag.com) is a website which calls itself 'the literary and humor magazine for expatriates everywhere'. It has masses of interesting travel and expat articles (it will even print an extract from your novel, as long as it is set abroad, i.e. not in the USA) and although it doesn't pay contributors, you can have the pleasure of seeing your name in print on the screen. *Woman Abroad* magazine accepts articles from its expat readers, and even pays for them (see www.womanabroad.com).

Setting up as a freelancer

Research your market

You can start in a small way with a few friends, using them as guinea pigs and asking their advice and opinions. Be prepared to change your focus to reflect what people want. For example, you may initially decide to offer a website design service, but find that what clients really want is tuition in how to do it themselves. If you are flexible and responsive you are far more likely to succeed.

Advertise

In Roundabout, ACCESS magazine, club and society magazines, international school PTA magazines, the expatica website, on school and club notice boards and at school fairs. Most charge relatively low rates for small ads, especially if you are a member. Remember that you need to be thinking a month or so in advance, because most publications have a long lead-in time. And regularly check up on the ads you place on noticeboards, to see that they've not been removed or covered over.

Look through the small ads

See what's on offer in these publications. Just because someone else is already advertising in your specialism, it doesn't mean there's not room for another (I remember one year desperately thinking up do-it-yourself entertainment for fifteen 5-year-olds at my daughter's birthday party because Mr. Magic, Crispi the Clown, Justin the Balloon Blower & everyone else I tried was fully booked that day! Would that there had been another entertainer on offer).

Network

Join clubs and societies and when you go to meetings, tell others what you have to offer. Connecting Women meetings have a space at the start of each session when members are encouraged to talk about their ventures and services; you can also leave your cards/brochures for others to take.

Make yourself cards and brochures

By doing it yourself you will not only save a small fortune, but you will also be able to make changes to your details without having to order a new print run. Most modern PC printers can take a surprisingly stiff card, which you can buy from any good stationer by the pack or single sheet, quite reasonably. Or you can buy packs of 150 ready pre-punched cards (*visitekaartjes*) for the printer from *Hema*. Even if you don't have very up-to-date or sophisticated software, it's still possible to make attractive advertising material. You can download copyright-free images from the Internet to brighten up your ads, at www.clipart.com. And you can buy special printed business stationery with colourful designs quite cheaply from Paper Direct in the UK through www.vistapapers.co.uk.

Get yourself a website

You can construct a simple website quite easily using the web wizard on Microsoft Word. No knowledge of HTML or any coding system is needed. If you have Microsoft Home Publisher as an additional program on your computer, you can build a more sophisticated and colourful site, again quite easily. Then you need to find a host for your site – it doesn't have to be a Dutch one (and you may prefer to look to your own country for a host; there are plenty available across the world), but you could try www.pdnl.nl (Stichting Particuliere Domeinen Nederland) for a convenient local domain name plus hosting. Dutch regulations on domain names ending in .nl are rather complex, but the site www.domain-registry.nl explains them reasonably clearly in English.

Alternatively, you can build and have hosted a **free** website at www.geocities.yahoo.com. The site has all the building bricks you need to make a really interesting and lively site, with very simple, step by step guidance for those with no previous experience. Again, no codes are needed. It will give you a domain name and host your site for you, but you are stuck with advertising banners. For a small cost Homestead (www.homestead.com) will give you a similar service without the advertising. If you don't like the domain name you get, which is usually rather clumsy, you can register one you prefer and divert your traffic through www.domeinplaza.nl or www.uk2net.com.

You don't need to have links to lots of search engines if you're simply using your site as a form of online advertising brochure, although it's generally quite easy to apply to be included on them – most have an online application which is simple to complete. You can put your website address on your card and stickers and in small ads and let the punters take it from there. If you enjoy making a website, you could even go further and use your skills to set up a freelance business as a website designer or teach others how to do it.

Stick to what – or who – you know

Unless you speak fluent Dutch, don't even think of casting your net beyond the expat community, initially at least. After all, there are plenty of international expats out there, probably just waiting to buy your cakes or learn hatha yoga from you.

Be businesslike

You need to take responsibility for running a small business, and that means visiting the *Kamer van Koophandel*, investigating regulations specific to your business and filing a tax return. There are several publications aimed at the expat market which tell you how to go about these things – the best are *The Holland Handbook, The ACCESS Job Booklet* and the expatica website. 22% of the women in this book have registered a successful business with the Dutch authorities and most would tell you that it is a relatively easy process, if a little tedious.

On a more general level, there are numerous books giving advice on setting up a business – e.g. *How to Set Up and Run Your Own Business* by Helen Kogan, or, if you want to take spiritual values into account, *The SEED Handbook: The Feminine Way to Create a Business* by the PR guru Lynne Franks. You can get a taster at www.seedfusion.com, a website dedicated to the SEED Network – 'a global community of entrepreneurial women of spirit dedicated to personal empowerment and positive social change'. Browsing on the Amazon website will bring up many more book titles.

Finally, don't expect to make much money at first

Unless you're very lucky – but it's a good way to meet people and to get established. And be persistent; if at first you don't succeed, try and try and try and try again.

UNPAID ACTIVI-TIES

4   Serving the community

Jennie's story

Jennie, 51, came at the end of 1998 on a 4-year posting with her husband, who is ambassador here for New Zealand, and also represents his country in the Baltic States, Norway, Finland and Sweden. Before coming to Holland, Jennie was an experienced businesswoman with her own company, a string of directorships behind her and a series of senior advisory positions, including special adviser to the Prime Minister of New Zealand.

When she first came, as she says, 'I tried to change the world on my first day! But you can't re-create what you had at home – it's a dumb idea. When I got over that hurdle I was much happier. I became more realistic about my goals and saw this time as an opportunity to change and learn and grow.'

Jennie has buckets of energy and has set about filling her time with all sorts of projects. She has continued to work with some of her former clients from New Zealand on a mentoring basis and still carries out some management consultancy projects. She has become director of special projects for Roundabout magazine and been responsible for promoting the latest, eye-catching, slightly quirky cover designs. She hosts an annual function for representatives of all the expat women's clubs, under the auspices of Roundabout, at the beautiful embassy residence in South Wassenaar.

She has tried to use the residence to help promote New Zealand ('The country is so small that people don't think about us'), by organising events such as poetry readings, wine tastings, cookery classes – for New Zealand lamb, of course – and fashion shows.

Together with other diplomats' wives, she has formed a kind of support group, which now has its own newsletter. The life of an ambassador's wife may seem charmed – no worries about finding accommodation with a grand residence available and staff to service it – but many are highly qualified professional women who cannot work while on a posting, and who do not have easy access to friendship networks. 'But you can't say, 'I've got all this and I'm still not happy.' I'm lucky I've found two or three really close women friends here,' says Jennie. Her advice to women who come at first is, 'Be your own best friend. When you're feeling under siege you need a friend, so be gentle and give yourself support. People are generally very happy to help you if you ask, but you have to listen and try put something back into the pot yourself by helping others when they ask you.'

Like many expat women, Jennie has taken the opportunity to travel in Europe. She has been fortunate to accompany her husband on some of his trips to Scandinavia and the Baltic states, which have opened up a whole new field of culture. In Holland, too, she has been exploring the art galleries and the cultural events on offer. 'One mistake I made at first was to treat the Dutch the same as New Zealanders, because they seemed so alike on the surface. But now I have made more effort to get to know the Dutch.' She has been learning Dutch and tries to use it at least once a week by going to the local market on her bike and doing her shopping in Dutch.

'Having time out clarifies your thoughts and gives you a different perspective. Each day that goes by, you miss opportunities. Make every one count. I want to look back and think what I've contributed and how much I've grown. I feel that all of this will lead somewhere; it's going to be useful.'

Jennie has lots of sensible advice for expat women:

- Ask yourself, what can I contribute and what can I learn from others?
- See your stay in Holland as a learning opportunity rather than a time-filler
- Don't lose your passion; it's very easy to lose sight of what you really care about, in the dross of the day
- Have the wit to ask and the compassion to offer
- Remember that life isn't always easy in our own countries, either, and most women are extraordinary in what they can cope with – and
- Don't feel guilty about enjoying life!

Sheila's story

Sheila Gazaleh-Weevers is a familiar name, as the author and publisher of the very best guidebook to Holland for expats (*Here's Holland*) and co-author of its predecessor, *Roaming 'Round Holland*. The story of how she came to be involved with this bestseller is an interesting one. When she came to live in Rotterdam with her Lebanese husband in 1970, their son went to the American International School. There, Sheila met her partner for this project, Patricia Erickson, among mothers of different nationalities and became aware that many of them were not happy in Holland. 'I felt it was because they didn't know what Holland had to offer. Together, Pat and I decided to do something about it. In those days there wasn't as much information available. I was a step ahead of everyone else, having lived abroad and here a while five years previously, and so I was more prepared. We gathered material from our family outings, practical advice and useful hints and distributed it on mimeographed newsletter sheets through our PTA. Other women were encouraged to add their ideas, so it grew and grew until it became a book.'

The idea of the book was Pat Erickson's. She wrote the original *Roaming 'Round Rotterdam* and, being the wife of a diplomat, was well placed to convince the City Council of its importance for newcomers to the city. But the subject matter – interesting trips to make and things to do – outgrew the title, so that Sheila published it as *Roaming 'Round Holland* in 1973, broadening its scope to take in the whole country. It went on to run through seven editions, taking up position on every expat's bookshelf. The Gordon Scholarship Fund, which was established with the very first edition, still operates and has helped many young people in the American International School in Rotterdam. Now it is in its first – of many, no doubt – edition as *Here's Holland*.

Sheila self-publishes, which is an enormous amount of work. 'I like to be creative and busy,' she says, with magnificent understatement. 'It's a challenge getting over the hurdles. The positive side of doing something like this, is that you work when you want to. The negative side, of course, is that you're never finished. It's only when you can relax that you realise how long you have been working and how tired you are.'

Sheila's advice to new expat women is to get involved, either through school if you have children, or through clubs. 'I learned a lot through voluntary work. The experience I gained helped me with my book and publishing.'

Doing something worthwhile: volunteer work

You may not be able to work in paid employment while you are in the Netherlands – possibly because you can't get a work permit, or because you have family obligations which take up too much of your time. It can be difficult to adjust to a non-working life, particularly if you have been used to working full-time. It's probably useless to say, 'don't feel guilty' – guilt is a woman's burden, sadly.

However, perhaps you can assuage your feelings by contributing something useful. You will probably receive a lot of help and support both from individuals and from groups during your time in Holland – you certainly will, if you ask and seek it out – and volunteering is a nice way of putting something back into the general pot. Or perhaps you simply want to keep busy. Working in the voluntary sector can be useful not only for those whom you are trying to help, but also for your own personal and career development. It might also lead to a job here, when you least expect it.

Volunteer work for ACCESS

ACCESS – the Administrative Committee to Coordinate English Speaking Services – exists to provide assistance to the English-speaking community to find services and to adapt to life in the Netherlands. They provide telephone information on Dutch lessons, doctors, music teachers, sports clubs, etc. etc. They publish useful information booklets – e.g. *Health Care in Holland* and *The Job Booklet*. They run courses and talks, and they have a referral service to qualified counsellors for those in need of professional assistance with personal and family problems. The website address is www.access–nl.org.

Sue came to Holland from Australia at the end of 1998. 'I wanted to get out of the house and meet people. I saw an advert for ACCESS in a school magazine and went along thinking I might be useful, as a midwife, in the childbirth preparation classes. Well, they didn't need me for my midwifery skills, but I was a bit taken aback when they asked me to take over the Community Education Department as manager straight away! It was nerve-wracking to start with, but I muddled along learning the ropes as I went. When I got a part-time job as a lab technician I thought I couldn't manage ACCESS any more – but I did! ACCESS has been brilliant. I've met such a broad section of society of all nationalities. Everybody is so friendly and the atmosphere is very supportive. I don't know what I'd have done without it, somehow.'

For two years Sue organised the courses which ACCESS runs to meet the needs of the community – courses on stress and grief and parenting. She booked speakers, placed adverts in English language publications and sent out letters of confirmation to participants.

Whatever your particular skills, ACCESS probably has a task for you. They have several departments, including fundraising, computer services, telephone contact and publications. A pool of at least 100 volunteers is needed to keep the organisation running, and each one pledges half a day each week (or more) to help in whatever way she can. It's an excellent way to meet others while contributing something to the community. ACCESS runs regular information mornings for those wishing to sign up as volunteers, where all the options are explained. Telephone 070 - 346 25 25 to sign up for the next session.

Vrijwilligers (volunteers) on a local level

Dutch people are well known for their willingness to give to charitable appeals and to volunteer to give help and there are many charities in Holland. An excellent way to become involved in the local Dutch community is to volunteer to help some good cause. Local free newspapers usually have regular appeals for helpers in all sorts of areas. Driving elderly/handicapped people to appointments or to the shops is quite a common one. Ask at the *gemeentehuis* (town hall) if your town has a *vrijwilligersbureau* (volunteers' agency), where you can register your willingness to volunteer. Many towns have a branch of the *Wereldwinkel*, shops which sell goods from developing countries at fair prices to raise money for charitable causes. If your Dutch is up to shop assistant level, you could volunteer to serve behind the counter. Or you could run a Unicef shop from home at Christmas, selling cards and gifts. If you don't fancy selling, you could contact one of the big international charities, such as *Greenpeace*, or *Novib* (partner of *Oxfam*) or *Artsen zonder Grenzen (Médécins sans Frontiers)* or *Lepra* and ask what you could do to help. You could volunteer to go from door to door with a collecting tin, for instance. Most of the big charities have a national collection week when this is allowed and it's an excellent way to meet your neighbours, giving you an excuse to call at the door of everyone in your neighbourhood.

Work for one of the expat clubs and societies

Most welcome volunteer organisers with open arms. High turnover of members means that positions such as treasurer or membership

74

secretary often become vacant. However, they can mean a lot of tedious and time-consuming work, so check out carefully what's involved before volunteering. But the benefit is that you can put your skills to good use (or develop new ones), feel valued and make lots of social contacts. Most organisations are very grateful, too, to volunteers who can organise outings and events. These take a lot of work, but you could learn a great deal from being involved and find out a lot about Holland.

Working with children

If you have young school-aged children, volunteering is easy. Schools always need practical help – with the PTA, in the library, at after-school clubs, etc. If your first offer is turned down, just ask someone else. Don't be discouraged. Your help is needed somewhere, and will be appreciated.

The Scouting and Guiding movement is always in need of volunteer helpers, and one potentially useful benefit is that if you have a child waiting to join the organisation, a place can usually be found quite quickly if you volunteer to go along and help at meetings.

'I listened to children reading, to help out class teachers, and generally got heavily involved in school life. My husband said I was running the school for free! But with one child in nursery and one just started school I had neither the time nor the inclination for paid employment.'

Jenny has a Ph.D. in biology and could doubtless find a job which used her special qualifications. However, she was brought up with the values of service to the community. Her mother was Chief Commissioner of Girl Guides for all Australia.

'Guiding was her career and she was my role model. I've done Guiding all of my life. When I came here in 1992 they were desperate for a Brownie leader, so I took that on, although I had always worked with older girls before. I also volunteered to help teach playground games at my children's school, and I helped to set up a book club which involved collecting money from the children every week and running book sales regularly. I listened to children reading, to help out class teachers, and generally got heavily involved in school life. My husband said I was running the school for free! But with one child in nursery and one just started school I had neither the time nor the inclination for paid employment. And anyway, I get as much out of Guiding as I put in – it's just that no one pays me for it!'

Become a citizen working for the Republic of the Web

The **Open Directory** Project is a huge, human-edited directory of the web, constructed and maintained by a vast, global army of volunteers. These volunteers each organise a small portion of the web and present it back to the rest of the population, keeping only the best content. Many of the major automated search engines, including Netscape, Lycos and Hotbot, use the Open Directory as a core service – you may well have used it without realising.

You may think that you could contribute nothing to such an important technological project, but it really is very simple. You choose a subject you know something about (Clothing? Teenagers? Movies? Biotechnology?) from a huge range of topics and volunteer to edit submissions from websites which apply to feature. There are clear-cut rules for judging the suitability of websites and easy tools to allow you to add, delete or update links. You could help to make the web a better place and become a recognised expert on your chosen topic. Go to www.dmoz.org to find out more.

Help to teach a computer to be human

GAC (Generic Artificial Consciousness) is a project aimed at mimicking the human mind in a computer. There are several such projects in artificial intelligence labs throughout the world, but this one is different in that you can participate through the Internet. Go to www.mindpixel.com and register. You are asked to present an unambiguous true/false statement – e.g. cats have four legs/cats have feathers – and then answer 20 statements which previous users have sent in. The aim is to have 2 million users registered by the end of 2003 and 1 billion valid statements, called Mindpixels, by 2010. The database will then be used to train neural net-based systems to mimic the human mind. McKinstry, the project leader, plans to give away shares in Mindpixel.com to contributors, so it may even be worth your while beyond the satisfying glow of altruism, you never know.

Become an unofficial agony aunt

It is increasingly common in publications with an agony aunt or advice column to solicit extra advice from readers. The Guardian newspaper is one such, and the BBC magazine *Eve* (also online at www.allabouteve.com).

You know the kind of thing: 'My boyfriend of 10 years says he loves me and will always want to be with me, but I only see him once a week and he doesn't tell me what he's doing the rest of the time. Sometimes I smell perfume on his clothes. What should I do?'

You could have the satisfaction of telling the deluded woman to finish with this no-hoper, smartish. However, often the situations are more complex and the writers may be vulnerable and need carefully worded replies, which suggest, sympathise and don't dictate. You might be able to make a positive difference to someone's life if you can write sensitively and empathetically.

5 Expanding your horizons

Catherine's story

Catherine came from Germany in 1989 because of her (ex) husband's job, with an 18-month-old son. 'I had always regretted leaving school early and I knew I wanted to study.' So she took an advanced German course at the Volksschule, and a TEFL course in the evenings. In 1994 she started on a degree course with the Open University and in 1995 she separated from her husband. 'I felt totally misplaced and displaced. But the course I was studying, Introduction to Psychology, gave me a sense of something real in my life at that time.' In 1998 she and her husband divorced, which resulted in Catherine having to take a year out of her studies.

'It's very isolating being divorced in this community. I was very surprised by the reactions of other expats. You're perceived as being different. My son was the only boy in his class from a broken home. I'm Irish, and at that time I think divorce wasn't even legal in Ireland. It was very taboo, very stigmatised. Going back to that environment would be difficult and I didn't have a family to go back to. I decided to stay in Holland so that my son could still see his father. It was a wise decision and not a sacrifice, although things could have been different for my career otherwise.'

Catherine finishes her Open University psychology degree soon and wants to get started on a master's degree, changing focus to human rights and development issues.

'My long-term aim is to become financially independent. But if I can't get paid work I'll do voluntary work. It's very difficult when you want a career but you're starting from scratch with no experience. I was a model before I married, then we moved to Germany and my son was born. But I believe in having a goal and pursuing it – what doesn't kill you makes you stronger!'

Ardis's story

Ardis (her name is originally Norwegian) came to Holland from the USA in 1985, when her 4 children were aged 2, 4, 6, and 8 years. Like many expats, she thought the family would be here for 2 years, but instead their stay turned into 16 years. She saw coming here as an adventure, but as an American used to lots of space, at first things 'seemed jarring and wrong'.

'It's like living in earthquake country. Like the people whose village has been destroyed by a Tsunami wave, or an earthquake, you want to rebuild things exactly as they were before. But another wave could come along any day and knock everything down again. We tried to make things the same as they were in America, but we didn't realise at first that many things are fundamentally different – for example, transportation. Once we got used to the idea that cars aren't necessary to get around, we started to enjoy walking, cycling and using public transport. You have to be very receptive, very open to new ways of looking at things.'

Like most women who stay here for a long time, Ardis has done many things. When her children were young she helped out at school, assisting on field trips, starting a lunchtime craft club, working as a teacher's aide. She eventually took on a full-time position as a substitute supply teacher, but found it unsatisfying always to be an 'outsider'.

Eventually Ardis decided to go back to school herself. She wanted to understand life better, so she enrolled on a BA programme in psychology at Webster University in Leiden. Her new qualification unexpectedly led to a part-time job teaching psychology for a year, a challenge she enjoyed.

In between times, Ardis has joined in activities at the American Women's Club and developed her musical talents through taking piano lessons and violin lessons. She has played violin in one of The Hague's amateur orchestras and is an occasional member of a local string ensemble.

With all four children now at University in the USA, Ardis is soon to return to California. Is she sad to leave? 'Yes and no. I've learned a lot here but I'm ready to have a new adventure. My family and our opportunities are over there – and the weather! I don't know the USA very well any more, so I have lots of idealistic notions about it.'

Getting an education

Do you want to expand your educational horizons? Change career direction? Learn something completely new? Holland is a marvellous place to be. Despite the fact that the official language is Dutch, there are literally hundreds of university courses on offer in English. Most are at the postgraduate level, but a small but steadily increasing number of undergraduate programmes is also available in English.

Nuffic is the official Dutch government organisation which oversees international higher education. Visit the website www.nuffic.nl for details of all courses in English, with hyperlinks to all academic institutions mentioned, or telephone 070 - 426 02 60 for a copy of their magazine *Study in The Netherlands* and/or a catalogue of all international courses in the Netherlands conducted in English (you have to pay a small sum for this).

A quick glance at the Nuffic website or at their publications will show a huge range of courses. Truly esoteric, the Amsterdam School of the Arts has a Master's Degree in Jazz Performance. Or how about a 2-week course on the artificial insemination of pigs at Barneveld College? But seriously, read on for some ideas about the possibilities for full-time study in English. The list is not at all exhaustive – there are many more for you to discover yourself.

The courses

Undergraduate

Utrecht University has a separate international English-speaking undergraduate programme of studies. It is called University College and it offers 3-year Bachelor of Arts or Bachelor of Science degrees. Specialisms, or majors, are chosen at the end of the first year from the field of science, social science or humanities. So, a 3-year psychology degree, say, in English would be possible. See www.uu.nl.

The Hogeschool in Amsterdam does a 4-year bachelor's degree in International Fashion Management, which looks very exciting. Participants become 'all-round clothing engineers' (For further information see also under Dutch culture courses, page 84-85).

Postgraduate

The Hogeschool in The Hague offers a one year Master's course in European Law and Policy, aimed at graduates in subjects other than law. This could open up all sorts of interesting career possibilities within European institutions. Half of the course is held in The Hague, the other half in Portsmouth, England, although it is possible to spend only two weeks in England if you do the course part-time.

There are many opportunities to follow BAs and MBAs in Business. Many of the 'Hogescholen' (universities of professional education) offer some form of business and/or management courses. There are also high-prestige establishments like the Rotterdam School of Management and the Universiteit Nyenrode, whose MBA programmes are among the most prestigious in Europe.

The traditional Dutch Universities offer a wide variety of masters' programmes in English. Just to whet your appetite, Amsterdam has an MA in American Studies, Groningen an MSc in Population Studies, Leiden an MA in English literature and Twente an MSc in Human Resources Development.

Development studies and agriculture are very well catered for – Holland attracts many students from developing countries to its educational institutions. And indeed, it has to be said that the majority of the 500 or so courses presented by Nuffic are concerned with business management or development studies.

Beyond Nuffic

However, Nuffic isn't the end of the story. There are a couple of independent institutions in the Netherlands which offer English language courses. The accredited American Webster University campus in Leiden, for example, has courses in psychology and international relations, as well as many business and management courses (www.webster.nl). The European University in The Hague (no website at the time of writing) offers business courses in English.

Fees

The cost of bog-standard bachelor's degrees tend to be quite reasonable – compared to other countries – at around € 1,360 per year for EU citizens (more for non-EU people, though). But MBAs and other fancy courses can command fancy fees, so check carefully. For example the Rotterdam School of Management charges around € 27,180 for an MBA, and the International Training Centre for Women (ITW) in Amsterdam charges nearly € 5,500 for an attractive-sounding 12-week course called Entrepreneurial Skills Programme for Women. Clearly, you'd need a large bank loan or a corporate sponsor to see you through. And the independent establishments such as Webster University charge considerably higher fees than institutions run by the Dutch Government.

Distance learning

If you can't find anything to attract you among courses based in Holland, then consider distance learning. British women will think immediately of the Open University, founded in the UK over 30 years ago. It is the major provider of distance learning courses across Western Europe and has a deservedly high reputation for the quality of its materials and delivery and support.

The Open University

The ou offers a wide range of certificates, diplomas and degrees in the fields of business, education, environment, health, humanities, IT, international studies, law, mathematics, modern languages, science, social science and technology. You could do, say, the Professional Certificate in Management, or a Diploma in European Humanities or a BA degree in Childhood studies. There are no formal entry requirements – the system is simply first come, first served. If enough students register for your course in the Netherlands you may be assigned a tutor locally, who will mark your assignments and be available for telephone consultations and occasional tutorials. It is more likely that your tutor will be UK-based, however, and you will never meet her or him face-to-face.

'The ou gave me a chance. I enjoyed social psychology – it makes a difference if you really enjoy what you're studying. It gave me something tangible to hold on to when I was going through my divorce.'

Catherine is nearly at the end of her degree course. 'The ou gave me a chance. I enjoyed social psychology – it makes a difference if you really enjoy what you're studying. It gave me something tangible to hold on to when I was going through my divorce. The TMAs* are worse than giving birth, though!'

* TMAs = Tutor Marked Assignments, which have to be sent in about once a month for grading.

83

The ou year usually runs from February to October and many courses have a compulsory one week summer school in the uk. Various Master's degrees are also available, but they have specific entry requirements. See www.open.ac.uk for all the details and online registration. The Netherlands local coordinator is Jane Ellis and she will send you brochures and answer your enquiries. Her telephone number is 070 - 322 23 35.

However, the Open University is no longer alone in the field. The International Centre for Distance Learning (icdl) has an online database containing information on over 31,000 distance-learning programmes in over 1,000 institutions worldwide – including 300 in the uk – at www-icdl.open.ac.uk. The database is easy to search using either their index or your own keywords. There you will find mountains of information on distance courses ranging from agriculture to personal development.

Free distance learning

If you want some distance education, but don't want to pay for it, there are **free** courses on offer at Barnes and Nobles' website (www.bn.com). Their 'university' has 8 'campuses' – literature and language; history and society; home and leisure; arts and entertainment; business and education; science and technology; health and fitness; life improvement, with a great variety of short online courses. The catch is that you usually have to buy a couple of course books from Barnes and Noble, but it still pans out very cheaply. If you're not sure whether distance learning would suit you, this might be a good way to dip your toes in the water.

Dutch culture courses

You could do a 4-year Master of Arts degree in Dutch Studies at Leiden University, where you will learn Dutch to a level at which you can then teach the language yourself, plus Dutch literature, linguistics, history, culture and art history. Alternatively, if that all sounds a bit excessive – perhaps you really only want to be able to chat to the neighbours and understand how a windmill works – there is a one year Dutch Studies programme, which aims to enable you to learn the language while experiencing Dutch culture and the Dutch way of life.

Utrecht University offers a couple of even shorter (four weeks mid-summer) courses: *Dutch Society and Culture*, and *European Cultures and Lifestyles*. Both are aimed at foreign students and sound like they might offer a good introduction to life here in the Netherlands and Europe. The Utrecht University Summer School also runs a one week course called Painting and Society in the Golden Age, on Dutch 17th century painting and 17th century sexuality and prostitution. Sounds fascinating – some of the Golden Age paintings are very racy indeed and all have a story to tell.

The Mauritshuis art gallery in The Hague has regular tours and courses in English, and The American Women's Club in The Hague sometimes runs lecture series on Dutch art.

Learn Dutch

The majority of expats come to Holland with a firm resolve to learn Dutch. Sadly, the majority of expats never quite succeed in this fine aim. Why not? A number of interacting reasons, I think. You cannot learn a new language well without a fairly hefty time commitment, and many newcomers have lots of other, pressing demands on their time. You also cannot learn without a lot of effort – practice, homework, exercises, etc. 'No gain without pain' goes for language learning as well as aerobics. Lack of early success means discouragement, which feeds on itself and leads to less time and effort spent, etc., etc. Also, it is very difficult to practise the language once you have begun to gain a little courage in speaking, because Dutch shopkeepers usually speak English and will often reply to you in English even when you address them in Dutch.

The methods

Perhaps the method by which you have started to learn is one that doesn't suit you?

There are several ways in which you can go about learning:

- Private lessons, either through a language school (pricey) or a friendly freelancer (advertise for a teacher, or find one, through small ads in your local newspaper).

- Group lessons, either informal, for conversation, or formal, following an examination curriculum.

- Language laboratory learning, where you work under headphones at your own pace, with a teacher who listens in and helps you occasionally (available through Nuffic www.nuffic.nl).

- Self-help courses, where you buy the manual and cassettes and work entirely on your own. Second-hand ones are often to be found at expat jumble sales!

- Correspondence courses, where you send homework – both written and tape-recorded – to a tutor and receive feedback in both media (see www.nti.nl under *Talen – Nederlands voor Buitenlanders* for one such course).

- Total immersion courses, where you go away to a residential setting for a week or two and speak nothing but Dutch, with teachers giving you lessons virtually non-stop (see www.linguarama.nl for details of such courses in the old Cenakel convent in Soesterberg or www.reginacoeli.nl for courses in another old convent in Vught).

These methods don't have to be mutually exclusive, but think carefully about which type of learning will suit you best and try to match your needs to what is available. ACCESS has lists of teachers and courses, and most expat publications carry adverts for Dutch lessons of one sort or another.

If you are in a group where everyone else seems to be more confident and capable than you, you will undoubtedly lose heart and would be better off with private lessons, at least for a while. But be sure your private teacher is both well organised with appropriate material for your level and able to encourage you through those dark moments when you feel that you will never learn this language. I vividly remember leaving one Dutch teacher's house choking back tears of despair after nearly every lesson! If that's the case, it's time for a change of teacher.

Some people insist that they do not want to study grammar, but only to learn to speak the language. I won't claim categorically that it cannot be done – after all, young children manage, don't they? – but if you want to learn efficiently and have a good understanding, you should be aware of the structure of a language when you learn it. All languages have grammar and rules, and all sets of rules are different. When you grasp the grammar, you have control over what you want to say. If you doubt me – or even if you don't – read *An Irishman's Difficulties with the Dutch Language* by Cuey-na-Gael (aka the Reverend J. Irwin Brown of the Scots Kirk in Rotterdam). This hilarious and bizarre little book was first published in 1908 and has been justifiably in print ever since, now in its 18th edition. The central character, O'Neill, is describing his attempts to master the Dutch language in a month's stay in The Hague. He bought himself some secondhand books to help.

> 'There was a fat little dictionary, closely printed, and there was a handsome new phrasebook in brilliant colours, containing conversations on the most unlikely topics. But I admit the Grammar Exercise book was the gem of the collection. It was printed on dusky paper, something like a blotsheet and bore the date 1807. It had six hundred and thirty-one exercises and contained many idioms, hints, exceptions, and explanations. In warnings, footnotes and asterisks it was particularly rich. Not a few pages were ornamented with nota benes of various brands, with hands, large and small, to draw attention to them. The English of this manual was very odd; and by and by I got the impression that the Dutch was rather shaky, too. Not that I guessed at first, you may be sure; but it gradually dawned on me.'

O'Neill is magnificently and misguidedly confident in his efforts to speak Dutch and ends up in a series of comic incidents where he unwittingly insults policemen and local dignitaries and causes minor riots in the streets of The Hague.

This is one of the few books I have read, which makes me laugh out loud – even at the umpteenth re-reading. If you know some Dutch, get the 'straight' version, as Brown wrote it; if you are just beginning, there is an annotated version with translations of the Dutch phrases. You can order it through www.nl.bol.com or www.abc.nl.

N.B. Suzanne Wensink's book *An ABC of the Netherlands* is an excellent introduction to Dutch language and culture for children (adults will enjoy it, too)

Professional qualifications

It is possible to study for some professional qualifications in English, through correspondence courses, while living in Holland. If you are bi-lingual in one of the main European languages, The National Extension College (NEC) in England, which is a non-profit organisation, offers the Diploma in Translation, which is recognised by the Institute of Linguists (www.nec.ac.uk).

NEC also has the British Airways Fares and Ticketing courses at levels I and II, for potential travel agents, and the Chartered Institute of Marketing's qualifications at either Certificate or Advanced Certificate level.

You could do the Engineering Council's examinations to gain Chartered Engineer status, taking part 1 and part 2 exams over 3 years of study. Or become an accounting technician through the Association of Accounting Technicians' examinations.

The Central YMCA Qualifications' Exercise and Fitness Knowledge Certificate is available through NEC for those considering a career as a fitness instructor.

Other NEC courses which are professionally based, but without leading to full qualifications, are in counselling and guidance, graphic design, childcare, technical writing, editing, homeopathy and book-keeping.

The Open University has a Bachelor of Laws degree, although it only applies to the law in England and Wales. They also offer a BA or BSC in psychology, which is recognised by the British Psychological Society. But in both cases, you would need to carry on with postgraduate courses after completion of your degree, in order to be able to practise professionally.

Computing and technology skills

What could be more marketable in today's world? Do you feel comfortable with computers? Can you word process, use a spreadsheet, cope with e-mail attachments, search the Internet, design a website? These are all fairly basic technological skills, but to the uninitiated they may represent a journey to outer space. This could be a great time to overcome your fears or satisfy your curiosity, if you can only find the right means to do it. There are, of course, local courses for the computer illiterate. Unfortunately, they either tend to be in Dutch or they are geared to international business clients, which makes them phenomenally expensive.

The National Extension College has a large range of IT courses, many suitable for complete beginners, on word processing, spreadsheets, databases, the Internet and PowerPoint presentations.

The Open University has a 12-week course called *Computing with Confidence*, taught entirely online, with teaching materials published on the website. If you are really keen, you could do the Open University Diploma in Computing, which consists of two or three modules and would take you at least two years to complete.

Cheltenham Tutorial College (www.cheltenhamlearning.co.uk) is an English distance learning institution which offers the International Association of Business Computing Certificate if you pass three out of four of the following modules: Introduction to Computing; Information Technology; Word Processing; Computer Programming.

The Certificate would take about a year to complete, by correspondence.

Courses in complementary and alternative medicine (CAM)

There are a few courses on complementary and alternative medicine in English in the Netherlands. Besides the Aurora Center in Amsterdam (see chapter 6, page 98), the Upledger Institute in Doorn (www.upledger.nl) offers a variety of courses in cranio-sacral therapy, although they are delivered in Dutch. It might be possible, in a small class, to ask the teacher to explain things separately to you in English, however.

Another means of finding out about English language CAM courses in Holland – or, indeed, any issue you choose – is to post a simple question on one of the expat websites, along the lines of 'Does anybody know of courses in massage/natural healing/Reiki in English?' You are quite likely to get one or two replies worth following up.

If you cannot attend courses, distance learning is an option.

The Open University offers a couple of general health courses that touch up-on CAM among other health issues. One such course is *Health and Disease*:

'This wide-ranging course considers the relevance of medicine, biology, history, economics, politics, statistics and the social sciences to today's important health issues throughout the world.'

Working for Health is another:

'This course examines the pluralistic nature of health and key aspects of health work in different cultural, historical and policy frameworks, emphasising a positive definition of health and ways of enhancing well-being in the face of acute or chronic illness.'

These courses can count towards a degree, or together they would count to give the OU's Diploma in Health and Social Welfare. They should give you a very good understanding of the nature of health, illness and the underlying issues. But they won't qualify you to practise anything, however.

The National Extension College (NEC) has a course entitled Introduction to Homeopathy, for those just wanting to dip a toe in the water. The British School of Yoga (BSY) (www.bsygroup.co.uk) offers distance courses in alternative health therapies (massage, reflexology, aromatherapy, etc.), stress and counselling, management studies, beauty therapy, writing and all sorts of new age stuff (runes, crystal healing, that sort of thing). I'm not quite sure how you do massage by post, but I'm sure they've found a way.

If you do take one of these distance courses that promise a diploma in some kind of healing within a remarkably short space of time – there are many to be found on the Internet – do resist the temptation to pass yourself off as an expert. Your diploma certainly won't be recognised by the Dutch authorities, and probably not by anyone other than the organisation that took your money to provide it. Just look upon the experience as another interesting learning opportunity, and move on towards even further learning elsewhere.

6   Fit and healthy

Nicole's story

Nicole is from Luxembourg. She started working as a freelance interpreter for the European Commission in Brussels in 1973, at the same time as Britain joined what was then the Common Market. In 1979 she started to commute to Holland at weekends to be with her future husband and gradually started to spend more and more time here until she got married. 'When I first came here I didn't even know that clubs like the British Women's Club existed – I just got on with living here.'

But Nicole has continued to work in Brussels for varying amounts of time, despite the fact that there is interpreting work available here in Holland. 'Paradoxically, it's more difficult to work locally. So much organisation is needed with children, that it was easier to go right away out of the country for a few days at a time. Interpreting is a very stressful job; it's not an exact science. Interpreters tend to be very highly strung – they live on their nerves.'

Nicole's daughter, now 16, is handicapped (she is blind and has a hearing loss) and that has made a big difference to the family. Melanie attends a special residential school during the week and Nicole is pleased with the provision, and with the medical treatment available. Melanie has had to have a great deal of contact with hospitals and specialists over the years. 'Out of all of the countries I can think of, Melanie is best off here in Holland,' says Nicole.

When Melanie was a baby, Nicole tried making contact with several Dutch mothers with handicapped children, but found what she felt to be a fundamental difference in attitude. 'They didn't want to discuss or share their difficulties, in the way that I did. Having said that, it's one of the best countries to live in as a foreigner, because people don't impose on you.' The Hague Support Group* was a help in providing a forum for discussion with other, international mothers of children with difficulties.

Now that the children are older, Nicole plans to increase her work in Brussels and expand her interpreting skills by taking the Dutch examination for the European Commission (she already interprets from English and German into French). Her advice to newcomers is, 'Learn Dutch. As a linguist I would say that, but I find that because I know Dutch I'm at an advantage. You can live here very happily without Dutch – in fact, living here doesn't encourage it – but it makes for a happier situation.'

Christine's story

When Christine first came to Holland via Australia, Austria and Germany (she is from New Zealand) in 1980, her husband's job was in Arnhem. In those days, relatively few people outside the Randstad spoke English and there were no international schools available. Christine's two children, then aged 4 and 8, went to the local Dutch school where they quickly settled in and picked up Dutch, having already learned German in Austria and Germany. (N.B., speaking with my psychologist's hat on, I must point out that it is a myth that all young children pick up a new language effortlessly; a significant number have real problems and can be very miserable in school if this isn't recognised.) This left Christine alone at home all day in an area with few international expats and no job, and – not surprisingly – she became quite depressed.

It wasn't until the family moved to The Hague three years later that things looked up. The children moved to the British School because,

* see page 102-103

as Christine realised, 'they were becoming more Dutch than anything. They spoke Dutch to each other and English only to me.' This can be a real problem for expat families who put their children through the Dutch education system. You may feel, from a perfectly righteous ideological point of view, that your children should participate fully in the culture of the host country, but if in time they come to identify with that culture more than your own, how will you feel then? A tricky one, that.

Christine saw an article about the newly inaugurated English Stream at the International School, sent off a speculative cv and 'much to my delight and horror (I'd been 6 years out of the classroom) was offered a job.' She worked there for 5 years before deciding to take a break from teaching (and from the marking).

In 1988, Christine went back to New Zealand for a 7-week trip, 'to find out who I was. I felt a bit of a stranger back in New Zealand – I didn't feel as though I belonged. The children had absolutely no connection to New Zealand and had become real little Europeans. It put my mind at rest a bit.'

Christine worked as an office volunteer for the British Women's Club for a while until she heard of the Open University local coordinator post. In 1989 she started working for the ou and continued for four years, until her husband's independent training company began to grow. 'It became obvious that the work was too much for Terry to handle on his own. It would have been stupid for him to employ someone when I'd be working for someone else. It was a wrench to leave the ou, but an exciting opportunity to work in our own business as an office manager and learning consultant. I'm fascinated by the world of business education and the theory of adult learning and did an MA in education while working for the ou. Our work is fun, but you live it seven days a week. We usually spend weekends and evenings working and Terry's away a lot.'

Christine has been here a long time and done a great deal. She lives life to the full, with golf and tap dancing and swimming and guitar lessons in her spare time. **'It's important that you are proactive in your search for work. Look for opportunities to develop new skills. Network. I've basically made all my own opportunities – I made my jobs happen.'**

In fitness and health

Again, I have to say that Holland is a wonderful place to be, this time for sporting activities. Although this is a small and densely populated country, the opportunities to take part in sports are widespread. From aerobics to yachting, you will find a club or a class to join. And if you are not a joiner, there are thousands of kilometres of walking and cycle tracks through wooded dunes, alongside the sea and in beautiful – if somewhat flat – countryside. Solitary activities make for great thinking and planning time. Several times a week I cycle through the wooded dunes near my house. I love to watch the seasons changing and see the trees, flowers and plants at different times of year. Some days I see red squirrels and foxes, or great spotted woodpeckers, pheasants and buzzards. It's such a bonus to feel that something I really enjoy is doing me good, too. Other women have their own favourite ways of enjoying exercise.

Jennie does **Pilates** once or twice a week. 'It's like an energetic yoga. And it's about a disciplined mind, as well as a disciplined body.' There is a special studio in Scheveningen, but since the only equipment needed is a mat, any gym or dance studio can accommodate a class. Jennie also does **yoga** and enjoys the social aspect of chatting to other women in the class.

Christine took up **tap dancing** when she noticed an advert for an open lesson in the local free newspaper. She didn't enjoy it at first – tap dancing is extremely difficult and she found her age (54) a handicap, not because of the physical activity, but in terms of remembering the complex rhythms and steps! – but rather than give up, she always thought, 'I'll stay for another little while,' and never quite got round to stopping. Now she really enjoys the weekly lesson in her small group and finds it a nice way to make contact with local Dutch people.

Rachel recently started going to a local gym for **keep-fit** classes once a week. 'Two neighbours said, 'You're looking so unfit and terrible, why don't you come along to the gym?' Personally, I'd have struck them right off my Christmas card list, but Rachel is made of sterner stuff. She went along. 'A lot of the women are lazy like me and not that thin, so that's nice. If you go in a group, there's peer pressure to keep going. And the group is growing because other women have heard about us and have come along to join in. In terms of integration in the neighbourhood it's a good thing. If you don't speak Dutch, most teachers will speak English to you if you ask.'

'The Dutch dressage scene is one of the best in the world. Entering competitions gets you involved in the Dutch community and you see a lot of Holland, driving to competitions across the country.'

Judy joined a British **sailing** club when her daughter came back from a school field trip full of enthusiasm for yacht racing. 'I would have joined a Dutch club, but they have a different system of racing. This club has handicap races every weekend and it's a great place for beginners, because there is always someone willing to help train them. It's not a particularly nice clubhouse, above a smelly cow byre, so it's just for dedicated sailors, but the club is a good jumping-off point for anyone keen.'

Wendy bought a **horse** for the family five years ago. 'I've gone from being the main rider to a maintenance-only role. I'm getting cowardly in my old age! I feel, who'd look after the family if I fall.' Wendy's youngest child, who will be off to university next year, has become passionate about the horse. She exercises it every day and enters dressage competitions. 'The Dutch dressage scene is one of the best in the world. Entering competitions gets you involved in the Dutch community and you see a lot of Holland, driving to competitions across the country.'

Jean has been going to **aerobics** for two years. 'For me to stick at it for two years is a great recommendation. I like it a lot. It builds up your stamina. It's for the over 40s – it's hard, though, but not too hard. It's the best place for me – a couple of weeks ago I went to a health club with a friend, but I found it too much. There were 20-year-olds there and I couldn't keep up. At our club we're all in the same boat, so you don't have to wear trendy gear. And the music isn't loud and 'in your face' the way some of the health clubs have it. I'd recommend it for anyone over 40.'

Fran started taking **tennis** lessons from a professional coach last year. 'I'm really enjoying it because I haven't played seriously since I was at school. I'm loving it and I've found that there are lots of other people who play too, so I can always get a game. Having lessons has brought my game up to a stage where I'm confident that I can say, 'let's play' and I know I'll be able to hit the ball over the net! I haven't joined a club yet, but I intend to.'

Sue got chatting to a woman after an exercise class in her local gym, who invited her to join a small group of friends and go **running**. 'I'd done some running before I came to Holland, so I started to do runs of 6 to 8 kilometres three times a week. The group had a fairly fluid membership, but it came down to a core group of four of us. The others were a lot fitter than me – I was shocked at how unfit I was; this was moving up a level for me. Then when the Dunblane massacre in Scotland happened, three of us decided to run The Hague half marathon to raise money for the children's charity appeal. That's when I started to take an interest in running longer distances.' In 1997 the other two wanted to run the London Marathon. 'I thought, that's a real challenge. I'd really like to do that.' Sue raised £ 700 for charity and ran the London Marathon again in 1999. This year, she has a place on the New York Marathon. 'But it's for the very last time. The training takes a lot of time and determination. It's hard.'

Sharon takes **golf** lessons regularly, at a course in Zoetermeer. 'It's a hike out there, but it's worth it because the teacher is so incredibly outstanding. I'm only a beginner, but he's made an absolutely enormous difference to my game. It's a very friendly course, a nice club, too. Being a Dutch club, it's properly built for the weather. The driving range is under cover, so your lessons carry on no matter what. I've had lessons in hailstorms, pouring rain and snow!' Sharon's 11-year-old daughter also takes lessons. 'She loves it. It's been wonderful for her. The teacher treats her completely differently to me, gives her individualised attention. I think it's a great game for children.'

Complementary and alternative medicine (CAM)

This is an area which is growing exponentially. According to New Scientist magazine, in the USA the use of complementary and alternative medicine has doubled in the last decade. In Britain, almost half of the adult population admits to using an alternative therapy.

As a bit of a scoffer, I remain sceptical about the effectiveness of alternative therapies, but I expect to be in a minority of one, soon. Certainly, among women who are feeling stressed and run down and among those searching for an alternative to their current career, many turn to CAM. The Aurora Center for Natural Medicine and Personal Growth in Amsterdam (Herengracht 607, tel.: 020 - 421 19 87) is a non-profit foundation founded in 1995 by an American woman, **Lynne de Jong-Decker**. She came to Amsterdam in the 1970s, around the time of the Vietnam War and inter-racial tension, in order to get a broader perspective on life. 'I felt like I was coming home. There's more to the world than the USA.'

In 1989 she completed a degree in natural health and therapy at Bloemendaal and since then has been practising holistic therapies. Aurora has around 20 teachers and therapists working part-time from the centre and they offer a range of therapies – massage, shiatsu, cranio-sacral therapy – and courses, in yoga, healing and tai chi. Lynne will send you her brochure if you give her a ring.

See chapter 5 for the possibilities of finding a course on complementary and alternative medicine in English in the Netherlands.

Eating healthy

The three basic words you need to know for healthy and ethical eating in Holland are :

- Reformhuis (health food shop)
- Biologisch (organic)
- Scharrel (free range)

Reformhuizen sell plenty of organic goods, of course. They also often sell homeopathic remedies (which you can also buy at the *apotheek* and the drugstore) and cosmetic items which have not been tested on animals.

Most supermarkets, apart from the very cheap ones, sell organic food. Albert Heijn is particularly well-stocked with organic fruit and vegetables, dairy products and meat. They also stock a good range of free range meat, some of which is organic, as well. These items cost more than the equivalents sprayed with chemicals or where the animals have been cooped up in miserable conditions and fed on antibiotics and the mashed up gruesome bits of other animals, but hey, what do you expect? And prices do seem to be going down as consumption rises. There are some butchers who only sell free-range meat – there is one in the Langstraat in Wassenaar. Look out for the logo, which has a curly green S above the letters PVE/IKB. If you feel strongly about these issues, you could join the *Proefdiervrij* (free of animal testing) association, which is a charity that campaigns – legally – on animal rights issues (www.proefdiervrij.nl). The Dutch website www.animalfreedom.org has a lengthy section in English about Dutch farming and is worth a visit. It advocates changes in animal welfare through legal methods only, unlike the illegal activities which the Animal Liberation Front promotes in the UK and other countries.

Your health

It is as well to be warned that during your first winter in Holland you will probably come down with various unpleasant lergi. It's quite normal for new expats to get sick with every bug around, probably because of a combination of their lack of resistance and a bit of extra stress-related susceptibility. It can be quite depressing, but it does pass and life does brighten up again, usually when the crocuses come out in February.

If you have a health problem in Holland and are unsure about what the Dutch system is able to offer, **ask**. Ask everyone you know in the expat community, ask your Dutch acquaintances, your colleagues, ask questions on the expat chatlines on websites. And ask your own doctor, of course. You may be driven mad by conflicting advice – and scared silly by stories of things gone amiss with other people – but you must try to get a picture of what your options are. People's expectations and experiences of health systems vary so widely, and sometimes we just expect too much. The ACCESS *Guide to Healthcare in The Netherlands* would be a good investment, too, even before you have any questions to ask.

Ebe: 'The most difficult thing about living in Holland is adjusting to the health system – especially for someone from a nation of hypochondriacs! (she is Italian). You must learn to move with the system and take the initiative. Don't sit back, but be proactive and ask, ask, ask.'

What disconcerts most expats is the 'handsoff' approach of many Dutch doctors. There is a Dutch verb *uitzieken*, which has no equivalent in English. It means – more or less – to let an illness run its course without any medical intervention. While many other cultures expect doctors to give medication whenever consulted for an ailment, Dutch doctors often have an expectation that the patient will go away and simply *uitzieken*. This can cause enormous puzzlement and resentment among expats, and doubtless causes Dutch doctors to roll their eyes at the unreasonable expectations of their foreign patients. But do you really want or need a course of antibiotics for an infection that will get better in a week or so, anyway? The Dutch nation is very, very healthy and Dutch doctors very well-trained, so don't be too sceptical about their effectiveness.

My personal experiences with the Dutch hospital system have been very positive (or as far can be, in the circumstances). I recently had an accident – relatively minor, it turned out – and it only seemed like seconds before a paramedic on a motorbike turned up, followed shortly after by the ambulance. The hospital staff were kind and efficient, I was given plenty of pain relief and I was dealt with very quickly. Eight years previously, I gave birth in the University Hospital in Leiden, and cannot speak too highly of the blend of handsoff approach with sophisticated high-tech back-up when necessary.

If you feel you want a second opinion, you could go to www.doctorbackhome.com, a UK-based medical advice site. An e-mail query will receive a free (currently, anyway) reply from a UK doctor within 24 hours, or if you have an urgent problem, you can telephone and speak to a doctor for a reasonable charge. This site also has links to other medical sites, including one run by the US embassy. There are, of course, many Internet sites run by quacks and charlatans and you must simply be careful and use common sense to weed these out when searching for medical information on the web.

Cancer

If you or a member of your family should be diagnosed with cancer, you can contact Cancerlink, which was set up to give information and support to English-speaking people in the Netherlands affected by cancer. They can send you a brochure (call Sheila on 070 - 358 82 84 or Pauline on 070 - 514 52 96, e-mail kellybp@xs4all.nl) and refer you to the *Integraal Kankercentrum West* (IKW) in Leiden, which also has information in English for cancer patients.

Mental health

It is not at all unusual for new expats – anywhere, not just Holland – to become depressed a few months after their arrival. You can call it culture shock (read Robin Pascoe's eponymous book) or exogenous depression or SAD, if it occurs in winter, but whatever name you give it, misery is the result. The really tricky thing is that it is difficult to recognise when you are experiencing it. If you feel angry, fed-up, anxious, tearful, pessimistic and lack energy, you should consider whether you might need help. You can do the commonsense things first – talk to friends, get out and join in lots of activities, give yourself a few treats – but if they don't make a difference to the way you feel, you should telephone ACCESS for an appointment with a counsellor, or go and see your doctor.

Your children's health

Helen came to Holland in 1982 with a toddler who had just been diagnosed as deaf. 'We came with a set of hearing aids and a letter for a doctor.' Helen rang every telephone number she could find in the phone book with 'British' in the name, but could find no help, no lists, no speech therapists, nothing. The first ENT specialist she saw said bluntly, 'You've got a handicapped child. You can either put him in a Dutch special school or keep him at home and read him English books all day.' 'I was in tears for months,' said Helen.

Fortunately, things got better. Peter was referred on to Leiden University Hospital, where the family was totally happy with the advice and treatment they received. The British School, under the headship of Mrs Jonker, agreed to take Peter in the nursery and he settled in well.

Helen met up with a few other mothers of children with handicaps. 'When you talk to people you realise you're not the only person with a problem. A group of us decided to set up a support group for parents. The same month that ACCESS started up, we put out an advert to see what would happen. We got some responses and set up coffee mornings once a month, started a newsletter, organised talks and set up an informal network of English-speaking professionals willing to help.'

The Hague Support Group is still going strong, although most of the original children have grown up now. The group celebrated its 15th anniversary with a reunion in August 2001. If you have a child with a physical, educational or developmental problem, there are regular meetings to offer practical and emotional support. Among the group, there is always someone who has experience of whatever child health problem you may come across, and they will be able to give you advice on what the Dutch health system can do to help you. I have known many of the women in the group and the majority will tell you that medical facilities for sick children in Holland are generally good. You will always hear horror stories about individual cases, but overall the standard of medical care is better than in many other places. Cathy Hart is the contact person, tel.: 070 - 317 51 01; e-mail hotcitygirl@hotmail.com

7   Home and family

Judy's story

Judy has been an expat all of her life. 'I'm a complete expatriate. I've never had a country of my own, although I have a tradition, which my parents taught me. I only ever lived in England for 8 years, early in my marriage, so I don't feel the same tug for my home country as other expats.'

As a child, Judy lived in Venezuela, Indonesia, Holland and Curaçao. Since she was married, 30 years ago, she has lived in England, Oman, Malaysia and Holland.

According to Judy, 'For a woman on the international circuit with an open mind, the world is your oyster. There are opportunities which would never be available otherwise. For instance, when we lived in Malaysia I became fascinated with shells and studied them in such depth that I became a real expert. On the strength of my knowledge, when we came to Holland I was able to work on a voluntary basis in the Leiden Museum and carry on with my research. Also while in Malaysia, recovering from a lengthy illness in 1990, I looked for an absorbing hobby to concentrate my efforts on. A friend had learned Delft-type porcelain painting in Argentina, and she taught me what she knew. Since then, my hobby has developed and grown to the point where I supply to a charity shop in England and take commissions. It makes me feel valued and useful. But I'm no businesswoman and only make enough to cover my costs. The real money is not in selling things, but in selling your skills by teaching others.'

Judy looks upon her pottery as just a hobby. 'My real job is helping my husband to get on with his work. We work together as a team – the best way of working is to work together.' Judy and Mike certainly work as a team in their garden, which is wonderful – see page 112.

Her advice to any woman planning to stay long-term in Holland is to try your very best to break into the local Dutch community. 'The expat community winges on and moves on (!). It's a useful prop in the short term, but if you are long-term try to join in with the Dutch. Even a little bit of knowledge of Dutch is useful.'

Sharon's story

Sharon was a tax lawyer in South Africa when her husband joined a company in the Netherlands in 1996. By sheer good luck, Sharon came with a corporate client already in place and she is able to continue to work for that company several hours a week. 'I was in the right place at the right time,' she says. 'If my husband's job had taken us to the States, say, I wouldn't have been able to carry on working.'

Sharon now finds that family matters take up a much higher proportion of her time than previously. 'I sat in an office before, happily cloistered from all this.' By 'this' she means the children's school and after-school activities and the general household management. Although she has a nanny/housekeeper, in South Africa Sharon was used to a much bigger staff. But she has no regrets and prefers life here. 'I find it a very civilised society. I don't live in a house with a 6-foot-high electric fence, like we had in South Africa. I can go out at night and not worry about walking the few steps from my car to the house.' She has become very active in the children's school, helping out with all sorts of activities, and in the local synagogue and organises Hebrew lessons in English for her own and other children. And the family travels together a great deal, taking advantage of the ease of access to other European countries.

Sharon's advice to other women is, simply, ask. 'It took me about six months until I found my feet. At first I kept looking for things that aren't available here; I went through a whole learning process. But I asked other people a lot, and I still do, particularly Dutch friends. We're not in their heads – we don't understand how Dutch society works, unless we ask. And I find people here very friendly and helpful, particularly the older generation.'

Making a home

Finding somewhere nice to live

If you are going to spend a lot of time in the house, you won't be happy if you're living in some depressing dump you can't bring yourself to call home. It may not be easy, and it certainly won't be cheap, but you should make it a priority to find yourself something special in the place you live. Make a list of the most important features for you (e.g. near good public transport; garden or yard; quiet location, etc.), then another list of those areas where you'd be prepared to compromise (number of bedrooms, size of kitchen, standard of décor and fittings, etc.) and go for the best you can get at the best price you can afford. If you have to be at home while you look around for something to do, or if you set up business working from home, it's important that you feel comfortable there.

Here is a horror story from **Jenny**, which I hope never happens to anyone reading this book. Her husband was posted to The Hague from Australia for the second time in 1999. Since the family had been here four years before and found perfectly reasonable accommodation very quickly, they weren't concerned about finding somewhere to live. Jenny was quite prepared for a small kitchen and bathroom and much less space than in their Australian bungalow – but not for the experience of being placed for five weeks in a holiday chalet in the middle of a cold, wet winter, isolated from both the Dutch and the expat communities, with no luggage from home, followed by seven months in a grubby temporary apartment. 'I wouldn't even let the children take their shoes off indoors because the carpets were so dirty. With hindsight, if I'd known, we wouldn't have come. It was dreadful. The problem was that at that time there was simply nothing at all available to let in our price range, not even unsuitable properties for us to look at.

'It was terribly depressing. That kind of experience makes you feel badly about the country and the people, although you know it's not really like that. We were lucky to find somewhere nice and affordable, eventually, by word of mouth.'

My husband's firm would not raise his housing allowance and there seemed to be no way out. It was really tough on us all – the children had no Internet access, so they couldn't e-mail their friends back in Australia and were miserable. It was terribly depressing. That kind of experience makes you feel badly about the country and the people, although you know it's not really like that. We were lucky to find somewhere nice and affordable, eventually, by word of mouth.'

There are at least three morals to this story. One is that you should take Rosalind's advice and ask probing questions of your employer before you come, and also use the Internet to check out the situation from the point of view of other expats. Make sure that your pay and allowances are enough to cover the cost of the kind of accommodation you need and that there is a reasonable choice of accommodation available on the open market. The best Dutch website is at www.nvm.nl. It is run by the association of Dutch real estate agents (NVM) and has details of thousands of properties for sale and to rent across Holland, with prices. It's a good starting point for anyone trying to get a feel for the current housing market.

Another moral is that networking is often the way to get what you need; Jenny's family found somewhere reasonable because someone they knew was moving out.

Thirdly, a miserable experience like this can colour your judgement about the country and all the people in it. Don't let yourself be swept away into projecting the misery of one aspect of life in Holland onto everything. Try to keep things in perspective, difficult as it may be.

Where in Holland to live?

When I first came to Holland, we lived in temporary accommodation right in the middle of The Hague. It was the first time I had ever been able to step out of my front door and walk through an area lively with shops, restaurants and pubs, and I loved it. Now we live at the edge of the coastal dunes in a very peaceful spot, far from any kind of commerce, and I love it even more. (In between these two, we lived in a rather densely populated suburban area and it seemed that no matter how far we cycled we could never escape from row upon row of housing. I found that rather depressing.)

Luisa used to live on one of the islands in Zeeland, where she found the peace and quiet blissful, and commute to Rotterdam. When she got a job in Wassenaar, she had to move up north to The Hague and although she lives in a lovely green part of the city, she still sometimes misses the islands.

Christine moved in the opposite direction, from near The Hague down to an island in Zeeland, when she and her husband set up their own business. They live on the outskirts of a village, next to a golf course, and have never regretted the move away from the city.

The important thing is that you should feel comfortable where you live and have access to the kinds of things that are important to you. When you are new to Holland, it's probably best to be close to the centre of things, so that you can meet people and reach the shops and restaurants and museums. It's easier to move out of town once you have already established yourself and know how to access the goods and services you need.

House beautiful

If much of your time is spent at home, you might as well make it a pleasant place to be, even if you think you will only be here for a short time. Many of the women in this book only came for a year or so and are still here 20 years on. Don't lose out on opportunities for a pleasant life just because you're temporary.

Dutch newsagents stock plenty of British and American glossy magazines of the *Homes and Gardens* variety. The smart Dutch interiors magazine is *Residence*, where you will find arty photographs of stunning houses and adverts for suppliers of all kinds of beautiful artifacts for your home. On a more down-to-earth and homely scale, *Margriet* and *Libelle* are two Dutch weekly women's magazines with sewing patterns, recipes and ideas for making knick-knacks for the house.

You could make a project out of prettifying your house. It doesn't have to be expensive. Shops like *Hema* and *Blokker* have a huge variety of cheap and cheerful vases, cushions, curtains, photo frames, etc. They change their stock frequently, so it's worth keeping an eye on what they have in, from time to time. Ikea has several megastores in Holland, selling vast quantities of home furnishings stylishly and cheaply. Market stalls are great places to pick up bargains for the home (see Shopping, chapter 9). If you do want to spend a fortune, that's perfectly possible, too, of course.

The Open College of the Arts offers a course in Interior Design by correspondence for those who want to move beyond finding some pretty cushion covers and take the domestic environment much more seriously. You could complete their distance course in ten months if you work about seven hours a week, covering every aspect of domestic interior design, with a personal tutor based in England. OCA also has two courses in garden design. The National Extension College has a combined Interior and Garden Design course, which requires you to complete 12 assignments and send them to your tutor (see www.oca-uk.com and www.nec.ac.uk for details).

Dutch cooking

Look at some of the great Dutch 17th century still-life and genre paintings and you will see a rich abundance of fruit and vegetables, meat and fish, and nuts and spices. The Netherlands was at that time well-known in Europe for the quality of its foodstuffs and cooking. These same ingredients are still plentifully available, but the reputation of Dutch cuisine has not really survived the centuries, in the face of stiff competition from France and Italy. However, there are some fine Dutch dishes to be made, and a couple of good cookery books in English to guide you. Heleen Halverhout has written *Dutch Cooking* and also a postcard-sized book called *The Netherlands Cookbook*. Hilary Keating's book *The Flavour of Holland* has some lovely illustrations and many excellent recipes. Also, *Dutch Cooking Today*, published by Immerc B.V. has 60 yummy recipes. Arm yourself also with a copy of *Food Shoppers' Guide to Holland (a comprehensive review of the finest food products in the Dutch Marketplace)* by Ada Henne Koene and set off on a gastronomic adventure. Impress your family with local dishes made with local ingredients. All of these books are available at the American Book Center, or they can be ordered online at www.abc.nl.

There is also a gorgeously illustrated little book by Gillian Riley called *The Dutch Table: Gastronomy in the Golden Age of The Netherlands*, published by Pomegranate Artbooks of San Francisco (1994). Sadly, I think it is out of print now. It has recipes linked to fine art illustrations and a scholarly essay running throughout. It's worth looking out for in secondhand shops.

Gardening

You probably already know, or feel, that the Netherlands is the most densely populated country in Europe (England comes second) and that space is at a real premium here. Many expats – especially those from wide, open spaces – find adjusting to the smaller scale of everything to be a real culture shock. Most houses only have a postage stamp-sized garden, if any, and often a lack of privacy. But even a 6-foot-square garden can hold a lot of plants, and in Holland you're in the right place to buy them.

Dutch garden centres are paradise on earth for plant lovers. Prices are reasonable (very much cheaper than in the UK, for example) and the variety of what is on offer is truly astounding, even in the smallest local nursery (*kwekerij*). The mega garden centres (*tuincentra*) sell everything to do with gardens, including furniture, ornamental tubs, fish for your pond (and the pond to go with them), tools, barbecues and statuary ranging from the smallest gnome to the grandest life-size goddess. At Christmas they have amazing displays, with Santa's grotto tableaux of moving figures and forests of Christmas trees, real and artificial. Xotus (www.xotus.nl) is a large garden centre near Delft specialising in exotic plants, which also has an Eastern carpets store and an ethnic supermarket selling rices and spices, etc. that are often hard to find elsewhere. It offers guided tours of the glasshouses behind the scenes and also, like most large garden centres, courses on topics such as bonsai growing or flower arranging.

You could make a project out of beautifying your garden, even if it is just a small rented patch. One of the simplest ways for you to achieve a glorious display in spring is to plant bulbs in the autumn. One big bag of daffodils and one big bag of tulips will give you plenty of colour. And you can write notes on your calendar to remind you where to fill in spaces next year.

In the spring, when you are reminded of how well your efforts look, buy more bags of bulbs, this time for flowering in the summer. Dahlias, gladioli and lilies are all relatively easy and quite spectacular. Trays of bedding plants – lobelia, alyssum, marigolds, petunias, etc. – are quick and easy for a bright splash. Busy lizzies always seem to do well in damp and dull conditions, and cost very little each if you buy them early in the season.

If you don't have your own garden, go out and visit public gardens. Both Leiden and Amsterdam have botanical gardens open all year round. In June a number of the Amsterdam canal houses open their gardens to the public. In May and June the delightful Japanese Garden is open in Clingendael Park in The Hague. In May, of course, there is also Keukenhof, perhaps the most famous public garden in Europe (certainly all of Europe seems to visit, if the numbers are anything to go by). You can keep up with garden festivals, special openings, etc. in *Roundabout* magazine. *Here's Holland* by Sheila Gazaleh gives exhaustive details of all of the year-round public gardens.

Judy and her husband have worked together on their garden for the past eight years and have made a beautiful, restful place. There are shrubs trained into fantastic shapes, trellises with trailing plants, a water feature, dozens of colourful tubs and baskets, a little terrace with herbs, a sunny herbaceous border and a long, mixed hedge beside the lawn. It's not a huge garden, but every inch of space has been made to count.

Indoor gardening

Surely every house in Holland has at least one pot plant in the living room. Go Dutch and get half a dozen. Or get more, and make a project out of dedicating some quality time to them. There are some very interesting plants in the garden centres, and staff there will always give you advice on care and maintenance.

Flowering pot plants, like the ubiquitous chrysanthemums and African violets, can be looked upon as long-lasting bunches of flowers, and turfed into the green bin when they have finished flowering. In December, buy huge red, pink and white poinsettias for spectacular decorations. Monster Swiss cheese plants and giant banana plants and rubber plants fill corners cheaply and effectively. Just remember to water sparingly, especially in winter, to keep the leaves clean, and to keep plants well away from central heating radiators and vents.

Get a pet?

To make your house a home, what could be nicer than a dog or a cat? Good company, needy of your care and affection – but a terrible tie if you have to travel away much. My cats have been cared for during our holidays in house by a succession of neighbouring school children over the years – one is a practising vet, now – and I know that there are reasonably good catteries (*kattenpension*, or *hondenpension* – for dogs – or *dierenpension*, for animals in general) around if necessary. Much as I would love a little dog, however, I do think you need to be at home a lot, both during the course of the day and the course of the year, in order to give a really good home to a dog. If you think you could, look up your local *dierenasiel* (animal rescue centre) in the telephone book and give a stray a good home. Some of the dogs on offer will be ferocious-looking rottweiler/ alsation mixes (why do you think they ended up in the dogs' home in the first place?), but you may be lucky and find an adorable pooch to take home and love.

Family

For some women, the thought of staying at home all day every day with young children – dearly as they are loved – is a nightmare. These women need at least a part-time job outside the home (and a good crèche or childminder, of course) in order to preserve their identity/sanity. Don't feel guilty if this describes you!

For others, though, having to become a 'trailing spouse' and give up work may mean a positive relief and advantage if it leaves the way open for more time to be spent at home with the children. Or perhaps there is no other, sensible option, anyway.

When **Ebe** followed her husband to Arnhem from Austria in 1976 with a 6-year-old daughter, there were no international schools and Dutch schools in the provinces were not used to dealing with children with complex linguistic backgrounds (Hélène was fluently bilingual in German and Italian, but spoke no English or Dutch). So, despite the fact that Ebe had always held senior posts in industry, she decided to stay at home and support her daughter through her first years in Dutch school. She got very much involved in the school and helped to set up a new cataloguing system for the library, then taught the children how to use it. She joined the PTA and became vice-president of the school council. She was at home for her daughter every lunchtime and on Wednesday afternoons. To fill up her time she gave chemistry tuition (she has a Ph.D. in the subject) and learned Dutch. Then, when her husband moved to The Hague, Ebe found a job with Shell, from where she was offered a senior management position at the European Patent Office.

The children

If you are pregnant, ACCESS runs regular pregnancy and childbirth classes. Their book *Babies and Toddlers: the ACCESS Guide to Having Children in Holland* is a book worth having. In April there is the annual *Negen Maanden Beurs* exhibition in RAI Amsterdam, which covers everything about childhood from pregnancy up to school age. *The Holland Handbook* also covers issues of pregnancy, childcare and education very thoroughly.

Depending on local supply, you may be able to find an English-speaking kindergarten, nursery or playgroup for your pre-school child. Within the Dutch sector there may be a local *peuterspeelzaal*. Do be aware that even if **you** need a break, young children don't always settle readily in nurseries, kindergarten, *speelzaals*, etc. And a Dutch-speaking environment may be quite overwhelming for the timid child whose language skills in English are still not well-established. A mother and toddler group allows you to stay with your child and have a chance to talk to other mothers while you are there. If you need a break, and can afford to pay for a nanny or mother's help in your own home, this might be best. Advertising in expat magazines and on noticeboards is the most likely channel to bring you a range of applicants. Live-in help can be found through the *Lady* magazine (see chapter 3, page 56).

Older children who are at school can still appreciate your time during the day, if you volunteer to help out at school and get involved in school life.

Or you could help out at after-school activities, or take music lessons along with your children, so that you can keep up with what they are learning.

One child-centred activity which Holland does very well is the *kinderboerderij*, or children's farm. Most towns have at least one, where children are allowed to feed and pet the animals. These farms range from a couple of grumpy goats and a few mangy hens in a muddy field, to magnificent establishments with horses and ponies in shiny stables and rabbits and guinea pigs which can be held and fed on little laps in luxurious wooden chalets. There are at least seven of these farms within easy travelling distance of my house – I know them all intimately – so there surely must be at least one near you.

Some children simply need more time, care and attention than others. Mothers of a child with a handicap or disability often have to spend a great deal of time going to and from medical appointments and may find staying at home a necessity in order to fit in everything that needs to be done. The Hague Support Group can be a lifeline for mothers in that situation. (see chapter 6, page 102-103) If you don't live near The Hague, consider setting up a group near you.

Third Culture Kids by Pollock and van Reken addresses the problem of the expat life and repatriation with teenaged children. They air a number of potentially serious issues, to do with adjustment difficulties, but at times I find the tone rather doomladen. Yes, some children find changes difficult to adjust to, but many more are quite resilient and find pleasure and excitement in the moves they make. Linda Bell's book *Hidden Immigrants: Legacies of Growing Up Abroad* also looks at issues of adjustment and is an interesting read. *The Holland Handbook* gives more information on children's issues in Holland.

Elderly parents back home

Middle-aged women usually have elderly parents, who may be in poor health. For expats it is particularly hard, especially if home is the other side of the world, to leave parents behind. A number of women in this book, myself included, have suffered the death of one or both parents since coming to live in Holland. It's tough. Make sure you have regular telephone conversations, and if your parents are at all computer-literate set them up with an e-mail address. And if they are not able to come and visit you here, go home as often as you can manage. It would be terrible to regret later that you didn't see more of them.

Family history: a project

One way of involving elderly relatives is to start a family history project. Have you ever intended to sort out the family photos? Now could be the best ever time to start. You could gather together a family history for your children. You probably have a baby memory book for each child – somebody always gives one as a gift, and it tends to be filled in with great enthusiasm for the first few weeks (baby's first smile, that sort of thing), then sits around inducing guilt until it is pushed to the back of a cupboard and forgotten. Get out the baby books and finish filling them in – as best you can, according to the number of years that have passed.

Then either make your own family record book – Dutch stationery shops stock a wonderful selection of large albums, with heavy pages interleaved with thick acid-free tissue – or consider buying a commercially produced one. Dorling Kindersley produces *Our Family Tree Record Book* and the Reader's Digest has *Our Family History: Record Book, Photograph Album and Family Tree*. Both are available on Amazon, along with lots of others. There are also record books for grandmothers (I completed one with my mother-in-law, an exercise she really enjoyed and hopefully my daughter will appreciate reading when she is older) and mothers. If you have a scanner, or access to one, scan in old family photos, print them out and paste them in your record book, rather than dealing directly with precious originals.

You could fill in and further research your family tree. Older children could join in and help, too. Before the Internet, this was not something an expat could easily do, without access to local resources and records in her own country. It is greatly simpler now than previously, as there are lots of sites to help you, and free genealogical software to download (see for example www.spansoft.org from where you can download Kith & Kin Pro). As you probably know, The Mormons – or The Church of Jesus Christ of Latter-Day Saints – keep genealogical records of people all over the world. Their International Genealogical Index database contains 750 million names! They have records available from the United States, Canada, the British Isles, Europe, Latin America, Asia and Africa. Their website is at www.familysearch.org and is a great starting point.

Julia – read her story in chapter 9 – has links to various genealogy sites on her website, www.juliaferguson.com, and if you type in 'family tree' on the Amazon website you will come across dozens of books on the topic. Family tree construction is absorbing and fascinating. You might end up getting in touch again with long lost relatives – we did, recently – and build up an address book of contacts in your family. And you can be fairly sure that at some date in the future someone – maybe your own offspring – will be very glad that you did the spade work involved in filling in the family tree.

On a simpler level, buy a postcard album and put in it postcards of all the places you visit with the children. Or buy *Kids Love Travel Memories. A Family Keepsake Book for Scrapbooking All the Fun Places You've Visited* by George Zavatsky.

8   Culture and creativity

Luisa's story

Luisa is Italian and has lived in Holland since 1983, when she came on tour from Sweden with a dance company (she has a degree in Scandinavian literature and languages). She liked it here, met a nice Italian-speaking Dutchman and decided to stay for a while! Then aged only in her mid-twenties, Luisa established her own company immediately, Gorelli Dans en Theater Management, which she set up in order to present and distribute experimental dance and theatre performances. She helped young companies – some of which are now world-famous – to find audiences.

Her work involved a lot of travelling and gruelling schedules, so in 1986 when the Ministry of Culture, together with the City of Rotterdam, invited her to manage a two-year project establishing a production centre for young artists, she was happy to accept. That project became Studio Al Porto, housed in an old gin distillery in Delfshaven, and it was such a success that it stretched from two years to six, staging forty productions, plus international conferences, festivals and other activities promoting the work of young artists.

At the end of 1991, Luisa had a baby, Vittoria. 'She was an earthquake in my life. I would take her everywhere with me, breastfeeding her backstage.' In January 1992 the Studio Al Porto project finished, when the subsidy ran out. During this time Luisa also split up from her partner and became a single parent. 'For the first time in my life I stopped.

Until then I had gone from one thing to another in my life without really making decisions – things just happened. Either I had to go on with theatre life or choose something completely different. I decided to go out to work, so I looked for a job.'

Luisa found a part-time job – which soon became full-time – at the Narwal Language Institute in Wassenaar, managing the language department. When her contract finished, she found another management job, as Admissions Officer at Webster University in Leiden. But although she enjoyed the challenge of her management experiences, 'There was too much paperwork, too much bureaucracy. I was too far from dance and colour and music. My heart was beating for something more free.' So Luisa set up Gorelli Cultural Projects in 1999, and at the same time started a job as an assistant gardener in a friend's garden centre. 'It was an adventure. I loved the combination of working with the earth and the intellectual challenge of doing project work. But I started to suffer pain in my arms and wrists and was told that I had carpal tunnel syndrome. I refused to let them operate on me, but I had to accept giving up gardening, which was really difficult.'

Now Luisa works part-time in an international children's centre and has focused Gorelli Cultural Projects on offering Italiano in Cucina courses, where she teaches Italian while cooking traditional Italian dishes at the same time. Participants learn to cook while speaking Italian, and then sit down together to share the meal. Her 10-year-old daughter helps in the kitchen and chats to the guests in Italian. Next year Luisa will extend the evenings of Italian and cooking into a five-day stay in Umbria, in the family home there.

Reflecting on her long stay in Holland – she never intended to stay so long – she says, 'I've only done things I really wanted to do at the time. It requires a lot of energy and there have been moments when I've had doubts. When you're a single parent you have to make an extra effort sometimes, but it's always possible to organise things if you really want to. I've had to push myself, to be open and listen to others. When I look around at how much is happening in Holland, there is such a lot of music, art, dance. It inspires you.'

Cristina's story

Cristina, originally from South Africa, came to Holland from England in 1999 because of her husband's work, although he had already moved here two years previously and the family had been commuting back and forth. 'So settling in was not too difficult. We had got to know The Hague and how to get around by public transport, and that was a help. Just the social structure had to take place after we got here.'

For the first year in Holland, Cristina was busy establishing her family in the community. 'I settled my son in to the British School, then set about joining organisations, mainly through the school, which had good parent liaison contacts. The younger your children, the easier it is to integrate. Luckily Edmund was still in the junior school. I enjoy the cultural side of things, so I also took the opportunities of what The Hague has to offer culturally. I bought a *museumjaarkaart**, went to the opera, bought tickets for jazz concerts and also, when visitors came I made an effort to go to things outside The Hague which I might otherwise not have visited. That's a good way of finding your feet. At first when you come you're a bed and breakfast lady. Our spare room was in constant use for visitors.'

Sadly, her father became seriously ill and died in South Africa just a year after Cristina came to Holland, and that took a large chunk of time out of her life. The death of a parent is very hard to bear and it is difficult for all the family, especially at such a distance from home.

In the New Year of 2001 Cristina felt ready to take on a new challenge. In South Africa, she had been employed by the country's largest wine company to promote wine appreciation, and had developed a high level of knowledge and expertise in the wine business. In England she had

* The *museumjaarkaart* gives one year of free access to hundreds of museums and art galleries across Holland. It usually pays for itself after about six visits.

worked part-time as a wine educator, developing and running courses through adult education centres. Now she is planning to run courses for the expat community in Holland. (Having attended one of her courses I can wholeheartedly recommend them.)

'You go through life from one stage to another and you keep on coming to crossroads. This is a new stage and a new crossroads – it's timed itself nicely. I'm geared up to my next 5-year cycle. I think it's very important to have time for your children, though, even as they get older.'

Cristina is also the director of a wine travel business in Cape Town, which she set up with a friend a few years ago. 'It's always on the back burner. I've done nothing to promote it or explore the market here yet, but it keeps me busy on and off. It's a flexible, portable kind of business, all down to e-mails and faxes, as my partner does the operational side in South Africa.'

Her advice to women coming to Holland? 'Try to learn Dutch. It opens up doors for you. Get involved with Dutch people – they're very friendly. Also, join expat organisations. Remember that thousands of women have been here before you and managed well.'

Taking on some culture

The Netherlands is a wonderful place to be for culture vultures. The Dutch take culture very seriously and every town has at least one museum, theatre, cinema and art gallery. Since nowhere is very far away from anywhere else, and public transport is good, it's easy to get around the theatres and galleries.

Read *Roundabout* every month for a comprehensive overview of what's on throughout the Netherlands (or log on to www.expatica.com). Music and dance is always well-represented and easy to find, but don't forget to look at the separate section on lectures. The Nederlands-England

Society and The Decorative and Fine Arts Society of The Hague offer regular lectures, as do various institutes and universities. Connecting Women (www.connectingwoman.nl) has a lecture on the first Monday of every month and ACCESS and the different women's clubs put on lectures on diverse topics from time to time. Most will allow non-members to attend for a slightly higher fee. As well as having an interesting time you might also make some friends with similar interests.

Books in English

When I knew I was going to live in Holland, my major fear was that I would not be able to find books in English. I spent months beforehand squirrelling away secondhand copies of novels from jumble sales and junkshops in preparation for the literary desert in which I imagined I would find myself. In fact, there is no problem. You can find English books in most major bookstores – if you have plenty of spare cash. The department store *De Bijenkorf* has a particularly good book – and music – section, with plenty in English. The American Book Center in The Hague and Amsterdam and Waterstones in Amsterdam sell books in English and many Dutch bookstores also have a section of books in English. But the mark-up on imported goods is high, beware.

When I first came, there was no Internet. Now, if I want to know anything at all about books, I browse the Amazon website. It has list upon list of books, all with descriptions and pictures of the cover, and some with reviews. Its search engine can find you practically any book you want, even with just a fragment of the title. If you use Amazon to order books by post, it's also worth trying the Dutch section of Books Online (www.nl.bol.com). They keep hundreds of thousands of English and American titles and, being local, their delivery charges are lower.

The obvious place to look for low-cost books is, of course, the public library. You will have to pay a fee to join, but all Dutch libraries have at least a few books in English and some have very large sections. The British Women's Club and The American Women's Club in The Hague both have excellent libraries for their members. Local Dutch libraries usually also have a music lending section.

Second-hand books in English are readily available at reasonable prices. Any expat school, church or society fair will normally have a book stall, with second-hand books at very cheap prices. In summer there is a Sunday book and antique market along the Lange Voorhout in The Hague, with stalls selling both antiquarian and bog-standard paperback books. The bookshop *De Slegte*, with 16 branches throughout Holland, has a huge stock of both second-hand and remaindered books, many of which are in English. It is particularly good for just out-of-date travel guidebooks at great discounts. It also has a good website (www.deslegte.nl), with a book search facility and ordering online, plus a book search service whereby they will try to track down any out of print book not currently in stock. Most towns in Holland have at least one *'witte boek'* shop, which sells cheap non-fiction books, mainly on crafts and travel, where you can occasionally pick up something interesting in English.

Book discussion groups

If you enjoy discussing the books you have read, join a book discussion group. Several of the international women's groups have these – although they tend to come and go, depending on the interests of members at any given moment; as I write, Connecting Women is resurrecting a defunct group at the request of several members. The British Women's Club has a friendly group, The American Women's Club in The Hague has a lively and longstanding group and the International Women's Contact in The Hague currently has three separate groups. If you can't find a group to join, then start one yourself by advertising in the newsletter of some group. The BBC monthly magazine *Eve* ('the smarter women's read') has a reading club, which you can join through the website, www.allabouteve.beeb.com. If all else fails, sign up for an Open University course in literature, where you will be guaranteed the chance to discuss novels at great length and in great depth and have your critical comments analysed – and graded – by your personal tutor.

Explore Holland

If you live – as many expats do – in an area of modern housing where there is a rather depressing sameness about the streets and a lack of attractive architecture or historic buildings, then it's really important to get out and explore the many charming old towns in Holland and see the better side of life here. Ancient towns such as Haarlem, Leiden, Delft and Den Bosch – and there are many, many more – really do live up to the picture postcard image of Holland. You can get an overview – literally – of all of the interesting places to visit in Holland at Madurodam, 'Holland in Miniature', in The Hague, where there are scale models of everything from Schiphol Airport to the Parliament buildings.

It's easy to find good guidebooks to lead you to the best places. Browse through the Amazon website section on general books about Holland and you will find 231 items on offer! Many are exclusively about Amsterdam, but all of the big guidebook publishers also have a Holland guide – Frommers, Fodor, Insight, Baedeker, Lonely Planet, etc. The best for expats, in my opinion, is Sheila Gazaleh's *Here's Holland*, as she aims her text specifically at people who live here. An unusual book about Holland is *A Curious Landscape: Foreign Writers on The Netherlands* by Gwynne and Peter van Zonneveld. It features extracts from the diaries, novels and essays of famous writers who have written about Holland over the past 500 years.

The American Book Center, with outlets in The Hague and Amsterdam, has a local interest section and also a website (www.abc.nl) where books can be ordered online. Their stores stay open longer than normal shopping hours and on Sundays, which is handy for working women. Waterstones, in Amsterdam, also has a good selection of books about Holland and most Dutch bookstores stock a few English books for expats, too.

The rest of Europe

While you live in mainland Europe, take the opportunity to travel to other countries in Europe which are easily accessible. Germany and Belgium are just across the border, and Luxembourg and northern France not so far away. There are good train connections to many interesting towns, and NS Travel (the Dutch Railway travel company, which has offices in most large stations) can arrange accommodation packages in some cities, such as Brussels and Cologne.

In summer the *Autoslaaptrein* (car sleeper train) goes from Den Bosch to many destinations across Europe, taking you and your car through the night to southern France, or Italy or Austria. Details are available from all major railway stations. Every year we go to Slovenia, driving for just over an hour to and from the railway at each end of the journey. We can pack the hiking boots and the roller blades and still have the energy to use them at the other end, without having exhausted ourselves driving for two days. It's a great way to explore large chunks of Europe with your own transport, missing out the boring bits. If you do have the urge to drive all the way yourself, the Dutch motoring organisation, ANWB, will give you free motoring maps of Europe and their shops across the country sell all sorts of useful accoutrements for the journey.

If you're not from England you might want to explore the land across the North Sea, or its even finer neighbour to the North, Scotland. Cheap airline fares to London are easy to find, and also to provincial airports – Liverpool, Glasgow, Edinburgh. The ferry companies also do good deals, offering 'mini cruises' to Hull and Newcastle, in the north of England (www.mycruiseferries.nl). The latest ships which cross from Rotterdam to Hull are very luxurious, and have even been compared to the transatlantic liner, the QE2! If you are prepared to get up very early, you can even do day trips to Harwich and London from the Hoek of Holland.

The American Travel Center in Haarlem (tel.: 023 - 538 03 58; www.a-t-c.demon.nl) specialises in making travel arrangements for the expat community. But any High Street travel agent in Holland will at least be able to provide you with an armful of brochures to give you ideas about where to go. Just go in and say, 'I'd like to go for a weekend in Prague/ Paris/Munich.' They will give you several brochures with a range of hotels

in the city of your choice, plus a range of transport possibilities.
So you could fly to a 5-star hotel in Vienna, or take the train or your car to
a humble pension in Brussels. You pay your money and take your choice.
The travel agent will do all the bookings for you and send you the tickets.
However, one complaint of the more well-heeled expats is that Dutch travel
companies tend to concentrate on the lower end of the accommodation
market. 4 and 5-star hotels are quite thin on the ground! Another is that
these packages, while very convenient, can sometimes turn out to be more
expensive than booking everything yourself. It's worth checking. But the
brochures are full of ideas of places to visit and make a good starting point
for planning itineraries in Europe.

Tapping into your creative potential

If you have time on your hands, take some creative classes. Music, dance,
pottery, painting, crafts, drama, all are available in English and in Dutch.
The Cecilia International Music School in The Hague offers lessons in most
instruments and voice, at all levels of proficiency. It organises concerts
and enters students for the Royal School of Music Examinations. See
www.ceciliamusic.nl. If you want to sing for pleasure, join a choir. The British
Choir (which is, in fact, very international) meets every Thursday evening in
Voorschoten (tel.: 070 - 347 21 44 for details). The International Women's
Choir meets on Fridays in The Hague during the day. Or join a Dutch choir –
most towns have at least one – and feel part of the local community.

At Studio Jean, also in The Hague, you can take lessons in painting and
drawing techniques. It's a good place to relax and socialise with other
expat women, but there can be a serious side if you wish – several of
Jean's students have done so well that they've gone on to have their own
exhibitions. The website is at www.studiojean.nl.

The Anglo-American Theatre Group is always looking for new talent and
behind-the-scenes helpers. It is a friendly group, which puts on several
productions a year, including a very popular traditional pantomime in
January, plus social activities. See www.aatg.nl for details.

The Open College of the Arts (OCA) is a sort of sister organisation to the Open University, concentrating on the creative side of learning, also through correspondence teaching. It offers courses in garden design; interior design; painting; drawing; calligraphy; textiles; sculpture; understanding art; creative writing; music; singing and photography. Visit www.oca-uk.com for details.

Mharie, who teaches English literature and language at one of the international schools, had decided that she wanted to take a part-time master's degree in literature in order to extend her understanding of her subject. However, when she investigated the options, nothing seemed to inspire her with enthusiasm (although you could take a look at the Leiden University MA course, if you're thinking along those lines yourself – the curriculum is rather attractive). Then she read about the OCA's Experience of Poetry course ('A writing programme designed to stimulate awareness of contemporary poetry and to help you to produce a strong and varied portfolio of work. It contains an introduction to the history, art and techniques of poetry as well as many examples of poems... your tutor will be a published poet, creating a flexible framework for the development of your own poetic style and vision.') Mharie enrolled immediately (OCA courses can be started at any time of year) and was delighted with her choice. 'I really love it. I'm so glad I did it. It's just what I wanted.'

You don't need to be a budding poet with a degree in literature to enjoy a creative writing course, though. OCA has a course entitled Starting to Write for complete beginners, or Lifelines – Autobiography, for those who want to put together stories from different points in their own lives or even write a family biography. For women at a crossroads in their own lives and some time to spare, this could be a very good means of answering those questions – *Who am I?* and *Where am I going?*

9   Finding friends and having fun

Julia's story

Julia had a strikingly unusual reason for coming to live in Holland, from California. 'I fell in love with a Dutchman I met online, at an international cyberfriends chat group.' She came to Holland in 1998 and married her Dutch partner a year later. Julia calls herself a 'love immigrant' and feels her situation is very different in many ways from a 'normal' expat who has been relocated here by a company and lives in The Hague or Amsterdam. She lives in IJsselstein, which is two hours away from Amsterdam by public transport and where there are few international families. 'The average Dutch person here doesn't speak English, and I often get stared at in stores.'

Friendship is a big issue for Julia. 'I thought Dutch people would want to make friends with me, but people here don't really grow their circle of friends, not like in California.' Julia's husband's circle of friends dissolved, too, when he married an older, American, woman. So Julia started a successful dinner group for 'mixed couples', to promote friendships. 'A lot of expat women with Dutch partners feel very excluded from expat life. There's a population of expat women who are really struggling.'

Julia didn't find it easy to feel accepted by her new Dutch family. 'I tried to over-accommodate the Dutch culture, then I swung back the other way. I felt I was losing my identity. You need to be true to what you are. I consider myself a global citizen – I love making friends from other countries and cultures.'

Julia joined the American Women's Club in Amsterdam, but found the travelling too much. So, never a woman to let obstacles get in her way, she also started the 'International Mixer Group' in Utrecht, open to all English-speaking expats who want to increase their circle of friends. The group currently meets in the Guardian Pub on the 3rd Saturday of every month, and people come from all over the country to attend.

Julia did have a job working for a Dutch company as a logistics coordinator for a few months, but now she works freelance as a coach (see her very detailed website at www.juliaferguson.com) and as a writer. She also does volunteer work.

Julia has found the website www.expatexchange.com a great support. 'That group really saved me when I first came. Also the news in English on the expatica website is a great benefit.'

Her advice to newcomers is, 'Develop a support system immediately and get to know other women. Remember that American women can also come from very different cultures. There's a big difference between New York and California, for example. Be willing to be vulnerable in friendships.'

N.B. Julia's website also has a huge, colourful series of personal pages on life in Holland (and life in general), beautifully put together. It has sections on culture shock, moving to the Netherlands, 'love immigrants' and what it's like to be an American living in Holland. It's well worth a visit for any expat.

Lisa's story

Lisa has come to the Netherlands twice – not so unusual for international women; there exists a sort of international circuit where families pass each other like ships in the night in Dubai or New Orleans or Aberdeen or Amsterdam. Lisa left home in England to travel to Paris in 1971. 'I went on spec and gave myself three months to find a job. I had lots of interviews and after a month found a job in the European Space Agency.'

From there she applied to transfer to Holland. 'I really liked Holland – it seemed a lively place. I had already been to RAI in Amsterdam to help organise a conference. I'd wandered around and took myself off. It was a wonderful atmosphere. I soaked it up and I loved it. I thought, I'd like to come back here. It still feels like that to me – I still go to Amsterdam on my own sometimes and wander through the lovely little streets with lovely little shops.'

So Lisa came in 1972. 'It was wonderful,' she says. 'There was a large crowd of us, all young and single, from all over Europe. We used to go out every weekend and have a whale of a time. That's how I met my husband in 1975 and I married him that year.' Lisa carried on working until Bob was transferred to Germany for five years, from where Lisa did an external degree in French and German from the University of London. Then they went to the USA for two years, then back to Germany and finally to Holland again in 1985. By this time they had two children, the oldest, Louise, with spina bifida.

A child with a disability needs a lot of ferrying around to medical appointments, physiotherapy, etc. and Lisa was absorbed in this for many years. She was involved in the early days of the Hague Support Group (see chapter 6), helping to create a self-help group for the parents of children with difficulties. She also had another baby and focused her energies on caring for her family. Louise had to transfer school to the American School at age 12, because the British School could not meet her needs; the other two children transferred eventually, too. 'I like the American attitude because they're very pro-children, very accepting.'

Although Lisa claims to be 'resting' now, she is busy as a volunteer for the school's International Transitions Program Team, welcoming newcomers. She also tutors some high school students in French. And she still has to go back and forth to England regularly, where Louise now lives and works, and where her elderly mother is in residential care.

She advises women to get out and explore the pretty parts of the country, or they may end up seeing nothing but modern, boxy housing. 'Full-time international workers don't really live in the country – they could almost be anywhere. Take yourself off and explore what Holland has to offer.'

Is anybody out there?

I saw a rather interesting little article in an expat magazine recently, called *Is anybody out there?* The author was asking for other women with the same hobbies and interests to contact her for some shared activities – visiting art galleries, seeing films and gardening. My first reaction was, how sad to feel lonely here when there is so much going on in the expat community. But then I realised how sensible she was to come out and ask openly for friendships. It isn't always easy to make friends immediately in a new place, although it is easy to find activities to join in. The original article has now turned into a regular feature, sharing information about forthcoming trips and activities.

'There are a lot of lonely people out there, who don't like to admit they're Johnny-no-mates. The dilemma is, how do you go about making friends? You have to be a little bit persistent. I'm fairly self-sufficient, but it's always nicer to go to the cinema with someone rather than on your own.'

I contacted the author, **Kate**, after reading the article, and again a couple of months later to see how the responses were going. She has a mailing list of 16 women who are interested in excursions to visit art galleries, although only a couple tend to turn up for each outing.

'There are a lot of lonely people out there, who don't like to admit they're Johnny-no-mates. The dilemma is, how do you go about making friends?

You have to be a little bit persistent. I'm fairly self-sufficient, but it's always nicer to go to the cinema with someone rather than on your own. I read an article in The XPat Journal before I came to Holland, about clubs and societies, and I decided to join the British Women's Club because I thought it would be a good place to go and meet people. Fortunately, I found plenty of women there who like a laugh.'

It's also clear from the content of Internet chatrooms and anecdotal evidence that there are some expat women who are lonely and unhappy. But it could be otherwise. It's perfectly possible to have a good social life in Holland, whatever your age and tastes, especially if you live in the Randstad. You know the standard advice from agony aunts for lonely souls who write in, wondering how to make friends? Join a club. Kate joined the British Women's Club (www.bwclubthehague.demon.nl) and has found a niche there, but there are dozens of other expat clubs around, ranging from loosely constituted groups whose main aim is to find a good pub to drink in, to highly formal and specific groups – usually part of larger expat societies – aimed at gardeners, or Christian women, or patchwork quilters or whoever. ACCESS keeps a list of English-speaking clubs and societies.

One excellent way to become part of a social set-up is to join a group whose aim is to produce something, so that you can contribute alongside others – e.g. a theatre group, a choir, a quilting circle. Another way is to learn a new skill in a class – Dutch, tap dancing, oil painting, whatever. Or join a sports club. Your tennis partner will have to talk to you, at least. You must persevere if the first places you go to don't seem to suit you, and keep trying until you find somewhere with kindred spirits.

Most larger towns have expat groups already set up, and the cities all have several. If you live in a small town outside the Randstad, consider advertising for friendly expat contacts on one of the expat websites, or even in your local free newspaper. If there is an international school near you and you don't have children (see list on www.sio.nl) ask about placing an advert in their newsletter or on the notice board.

'Foreign friends'

Foreign Friends is a company, run by two women friends, which arranges social outings and excursions in English for expats. They offer a variety of activities, such as boat trips, theatre visits, roller-blading in Amsterdam or golf lessons. All of the events involve a meal or snack, so that the expat participants can get to know each other better. See www.foreignfriends.nl for details of forthcoming events and prices.

'Don't be dismayed if you find it difficult to connect with Dutch friends. Dutch people have been taught not to stand out, so they can be slow to commit themselves to someone different.'

Dutch friends

Women who come to live in Holland from other countries often have a powerful desire to make Dutch friends. Equally often they end up feeling disappointed. Be realistic and take your friends where you find them. Most Dutch women have a firmly established network of family, social acquaintances and old school friends. They are not sitting around waiting for a gap in their lives to be filled by you. They will be friendly to you as neighbours, of course – I have a good over-the-garden-fence relationship with all of the women in my street, and occasionally some of us have coffee together – but the social web of their lives will already have been woven and you shouldn't expect otherwise. I find that the Dutch women with whom I have the easiest relationships are those who have themselves lived as expats or who have some link to the international community, either through a non-Dutch partner or through their work.

Lynne, who has been here for 30 years and has a Dutch husband, advises looking hard for kindred spirits in the international community. 'Don't try to fit into the Dutch world – it's very different and it has its own rules. Don't be dismayed if you find it difficult to connect with Dutch friends. Dutch people have been taught not to stand out, so they can be slow to commit themselves to someone different.'

However, **Tracy**, from the USA, is keen to be friendly and involved in her neighbourhood. As well as organising and participating in pot luck suppers, and the annual family day in the local park, this year she and her husband are organising a neighbourhood golf tournament, with a 19th hole celebration and dinner afterwards. As she says in her flier, 'This event provides an excellent opportunity for those of us who live in close proximity...to get together for a day of fun and good neighbourhood spirit.'

If you do want to pursue the idea of Dutch friendships, then one of the easiest ways is to join a group – an evening class, a choir, a sports club – and see what develops from there. But then it goes without saying that you **must** learn to speak Dutch reasonably well. Although the majority of Dutch people are perfectly willing and able to converse with you in English, in the longer term it's simply not good manners to expect this as of right. And you will feel excluded from the general conversation if a discussion is taking place in Dutch.

Make a plan

If you find yourself becoming reclusive and turning into the kind of stay-at-home partner you never wanted to be, be firm with yourself. Make a long list of possible things to do, sign up for the appropriate classes and groups and then write your weekly timetable – e.g.

	Mon	Tues	Wed	Thurs	Fri
A.M.	Open University study	Open University study	Open University study	Open University study	Dutch lesson
P.M.	Jogging Painting class	Tennis Give tuition to student	Jogging Meet friends for coffee	Swimming Give tuition to student	Jogging Voluntary work

And stick to it. At the very least you will be busy and find that time passes quickly. At best, you may find that one or two of your activities become so absorbing that you expand the time you spend on them and develop a really meaningful commitment, and make some friends along the way.

As an expat, you may find yourself approached by a group called **Landmark Education**, based in Amsterdam. This is a worldwide organisation, originating in the USA, whose aim is to enable you to 'live life more fully'. It operates through a programme, or curriculum, of 3½ day intensive seminars, in English, during which participants are led to develop breakthroughs in their personal awareness and understanding. I was invited to an introductory evening presentation by **Rosemary** and went along out of curiosity. When I got home, I checked out Landmark on the Internet and found a number of sites, including www.rickross.com/groups/landmark.html, which gives a very negative picture of the organisation. To balance out the picture, I also found another site which exists to give the positive side of the Landmark picture (www.scooponlandmarkforum.com). In contrast, it has testimonials from people who have been involved with Landmark and loved it. And I should point out that Rosemary has found the courses enormously helpful in her personal life. What Landmark offers – improved relationships and personal effectiveness, better communication skills, the ability to live life to the full – is surely what we all want. But is it simply Motherhood and Apple Pie? Common sense cloaked in mystical terms? Or something much more difficult to cope with?

If **you** are invited to join an introductory talk or a seminar – and you have to be personally invited, since there is no public recruitment through advertising – do check out the Internet first and go into it, if you will, with your eyes wide open. You may make friends and meet people, and you may find benefits in your personal life – but you may find it otherwise.

Finding Faith

Many women find comfort and support in their religious beliefs when they find themselves in difficult situations. There are English-speaking churches of practically every denomination in Holland, and lists of these are easily found from ACCESS or on the Internet. One spin-off of joining a church group is the fellowship and friendships which develop from being a member. **Rosemary** found support from the Unitarian Universalist fellowship. **Florence** attends the American Protestant Church, **Norma** enjoys the multicultural aspects of the Scots International Church in Rotterdam, with its 43 nationalities, and **Sharon** is heavily involved in the Synagogue. You are likely to gain support in both practical and emotional ways from the congregation. It works both ways, though. You will also be able to offer support to others less fortunate, through the charitable work which practically every church carries out.

Gerry attends the monthly Christian Viewpoint meetings for women regularly. 'I don't go to church, and I'm not religious, but I enjoy the meetings. They're not Bible-bashers – don't be frightened off by the name. They're very friendly and welcoming and if you're in need of help and need somebody to talk to, they're there. It's a social group and they have interesting speakers and activities. They always say, if you know someone new to the community, bring them along and they'll be welcome.' (Contact Margaret Blacker on 070 - 514 13 34).

Having fun

Pubbing and clubbing

If you are young enough – or old and energetic enough – to go clubbing, Holland has plenty to offer, in the main cities at least. There is no point in recommending specific pubs and clubs, as the nature of these places is that this month's hot spot is next month's dead duck. What you must do is find some likeminded mates to go out with, and let them show you where to go this Saturday night. If you have no readymade friends, then the best place to start is with one of the expat societies open to both sexes, which run pub nights – for example The British Society of Amsterdam (www.britishsocietyofamsterdam.org), or Julia's International Mixer Group in Utrecht (see page 129).

Retail therapy

A bit of retail therapy could do you the world of good if you're feeling low.
With a full wallet, shopping can be paradise in Holland. There are countless
neat little boutiques selling everything from antiques to designer dresses.
Most towns and cities have at least one street where the smart shops are
congregated, worth some serious window shopping at least. At special
times of year – Christmas, Easter, the Queen's Birthday – Dutch window
displays are a real visual treat.

However, you may not be so flush. There is still fun to be had, though.
Most Dutch towns have a weekly general market, with stalls selling fresh
produce and a range of consumer durables. There are usually buttons,
lace and ribbons by the centimetre, pet food supplies, socks, furnishing
materials, greetings cards, doormats and kitchen utensils. But you can
find almost anything, depending on which stalls happen to be set up on a
particular day. The biggest general market in Holland – so they claim – is in
The Hague, on the Hobbemaplein, held on Mondays, Wednesdays, Fridays
and Saturdays. Judge Mumba (chapter 2) found it difficult to adapt to
eating Dutch food at first, but then she discovered that The Hague market
sells dried fish and other food items just like at home and food shopping
became easier. It certainly has a huge range of stalls and is particularly
good on ethnic produce from countries outside Europe. The smells are
fantastic – and the prices are fantastically cheap. An even greater claim,
to be the biggest indoor market in Europe, is made by the '*Zwarte Markt*'
at Beverwijk. It is open Saturdays and Sundays and is patently on a grand
scale, with over 3,000 stalls and 55 eating places.

Many women find it particularly trying if they cannot find the foodstuffs
that they – or more likely, their finicky partners and children – are used to
back home. *Food Shoppers' Guide to Holland (a comprehensive review of
the finest food products in the Dutch Marketplace)* by Ada Henne Koene is
a great book to help you pinpoint suppliers and alternatives to what you
are looking for. It is thorough and well-researched. If you are here for a
long time, however, you will probably come to accept life without lime
marmalade or Cheerios, if you can't find an obscure little supplier

somewhere. In their early days of expat life, people tend to return from trips home with suitcases bulging with edible goodies, but as time goes on they find that it simply isn't worth the candle and give in to a diet of *vla* and *spek* (just joking; Holland does have an excellent range of fresh food readily available – see chapter 6 for details of how to find *really* healthy food, and chapter 7 for details of cookery books).

In Amsterdam you will find a number of specialised markets – for art, antiques, books, birds, flowers, organic food, stamps and textiles. Other towns and cities also have specialised markets, and there are regular *beurzen*, or fairs, which take place in large halls and congress centres across the country. For example, in RAI Amsterdam there is the Huishoudbeurs in March each year, and also in March is the Expat Fair in Nieuwegein near Utrecht. The European Fine Art Fair in Maastricht (TEFAF) in March is Europe's biggest and most prestigious antiques and art fair, and a wonderful spectacle, even if there is nothing actually affordable for sale. See www.tefaf.com for details.

Moving on from the sublime, The Darling Market in Rijswijk (www.darling.nl) has a *neuzelbeurs* on the first weekend of the month, where individuals and families can set up stalls to sell their secondhand junk. On the second weekend of the month it's called a *budgetbeurs*, and commercial enterprises are allowed to join in, too. It's a great place to rummage around for bargains. On the other weekends it features a variety of different fairs. Sometimes it's dolls and dollhouses, sometimes minerals and precious stones, sometimes '50s paraphernalia, or the paranormal, or sex aids. Something for everyone, really, although if you did attend the sex show you probably wouldn't want to bump into other members of your tennis club there.

If you need to shop and really don't enjoy going out, there is always the trusty Internet, with a thousand and one retailers desperate to sell you everything from DVD players to French knickers. An alternative to online shopping is catalogue shopping. Lots of women in Holland – myself included – have the *Neckermann* catalogue, a 2-inch thick glossy emporium of clothing and household goods. At least you can flick through it in bed, unlike a website. It's slightly old-fashioned, but has good sales twice a year (30% off all clothes), and it often stocks things, like awkward-sized tablecloths, that are difficult to find elsewhere. You can pay on extended credit, too. Ordering – and sending back goods which don't suit – is very simple indeed. Look at the website, www.neckermann.nl to order a catalogue.

10 Decisions, dilemmas and words of wisdom

Jan's story

Jan came to Holland in 1985 with her first husband, who had taken on a job with a Dutch company. Their baby had her first birthday on the day that they moved. Less than two years later, her husband was dead, of meningitis, leaving Jan a widow at 30 with two babies. She had to decide whether to stay or go back to England. 'I don't know why I stayed, really. Your mind is like treacle at that point. My dad said, come home and we'll take care of you, but I'd lived away from home for 12 years and I didn't want to go back. 'I'll stay for now,' I thought and just tried to get on with things.'

Jan was introduced by a mutual friend to Richard, whose wife had just died, leaving him with three young children. Initially, they helped each other through the red tape and legal bureaucracy that surrounds a death, then started going out together casually. 'After about a year something clicked. I suppose it sounds like a fairy tale.' Jan and Richard were married in 1990 and became a family of five young children. 'It was very hectic. All five children were very close in age. In the early years I concentrated on the family, through necessity really. But there comes a point when you want something for yourself. I wanted something that enabled me to be here for the children.'

Jan had done a hobby course in stained glass ('I did go to art school for four years and that helped, but it was a long time ago') and started to work with Tiffany-style pieces. During the past six years she has developed her glass work, designing and selling beautiful leaded panels.

She has held exhibitions, completed commissions and has recently acquired a new kiln, which has allowed her to move into glass dishes and other smaller pieces. Now she feels ready to take professional training at a higher level and is investigating the possibilities. 'I think I'm moving on in my work, but I'm in two minds about leaving the family, even now.'

Norma's story

Norma had been a paediatric nurse in Scotland before she came to Holland in 1982, because of her husband's job. Although she had a young baby with her, who had been premature and quite poorly, Norma managed to carry on with her Open University degree, after a year's break. 'I had a horror of turning into a 'Persil housewife' – I was determined not to be just a wife.'

In 1985 Norma had her second baby, also premature and very, very sick. 'When you have a sick child overseas you don't have the family support. The family back home feel guilty and helpless, so you don't tell them so much. It's scary going into hospital in an emergency situation when it's not your language and culture. Rebecca was in and out of hospital for eight years, with pneumonia so many times and three episodes of septicaemia. There was nobody from home to help us, but The Hague Support Group* was a great help. You realise that there are people worse off than you.'

Despite having to devote lots of time and energy to Rebecca, Norma completed a BA Honours in History, awarded by the Open University in 1987. In 1994 she completed a TEFL qualification. 'I was very keen not to do it as a little hobby thing. I wanted a range of teaching experience.' Her first job was teaching a group of Indonesian diesel engineers at Leiden University. She worked with a group of women teachers, all part-time, who were able to organise the work schedules together around their childcare needs.

* see chapter 6, page 102-103

Since then, Norma has taught many different groups of adults and children. She currently works part-time at one of the Dutch international schools, assessing the needs of children at intake. She also teaches English to *Dienst over grens* adults who are about to go and work in developing countries. And, in addition, she has set up a business called Expressions, together with a friend, to provide English language courses for companies with specific needs. 'It took longer than we thought to get going (although they only started a year ago), but business is building up and now we have a foot in the door of a big multinational organisation. I love teaching – I absolutely love it and I'd never have done it if we hadn't come here.'

Norma is very happy in Holland. When her husband talked about returning home recently, she was perturbed. 'I thought, I'm not ready to go. Why do I need to go back? My husband felt uncomfortable knowing that if he trailed me back there would be a lot less for me in Scotland. So we bought a smaller, more flexible house in Leiden, so that we can commute if we want, and rent out part of the house. It was a novel way of resolving our dilemma.' With both girls having left home now, it seems an ideal solution for Norma, to live flexibly between two countries.

To stay or not to stay?

Most women who come to Holland with their partners have little choice as to when and whether they leave again. Some are glad to go back home or move on to a new country, but others leave with very heavy hearts. Some women, though, do have a choice, albeit in difficult circumstances.

Jan, whose story begins this chapter, decided to stay when her husband died, as did **Sheila,** whose story is at the start of chapter 8. Sheila's husband died from cancer at the age of 40, leaving her with a young son. Both women wanted to have some stability in their own and their children's lives at a time of personal tragedy. Both have been glad that they made that decision. **Catherine** (see her story at the start of chapter 5) also decided to stay for the sake of her son, when she and her husband divorced.

Kathy was divorced recently, about a year after her marriage broke down. 'I thought about going back home to England,' she said. 'My family are there and my mum has been incredibly supportive to me throughout the separation and divorce. But my two children are very happy and settled here at school and I think they need some stability just now. We've lived in Holland for 12 years and I have a good job, which I enjoy. It means that I can just about manage financially to buy out my ex-husband's share of our house. Also, the children will see their father regularly and we all think that's very important.'

Kathy was impressed with the speed at which the Dutch legal system handled the divorce and the custody issues. 'It all went very smoothly and amicably. I can't imagine having the same experience in an English court.'

'I found both the school and Holland very, very easy to settle in to. The school was a small, caring community and everybody bent over backwards to help you. I found Holland a very easy country to live in – after I got over the culture shock of Albert Heijn!'

Initially, **Sandra** also decided to stay in similar circumstances. However, her husband's behaviour (he had walked out on her, leaving her with their three young children, claiming – to Sandra's astonishment – that their marriage was a sham and that he had never loved her; now he had found his true love and was going to live with her) became so extreme and provocative over the custody of their children and financial support, that she decided the only sensible option was to return to the UK with the children and get a job there. Fortunately, she was offered the first job she applied for – one she was really keen on getting, to boot – despite having been out of the job market for eight years while bringing up a young family. Although she is very sad to leave Holland and feels that she has been driven out, she will be living closer to her family, who will be able to offer her support.

Rachel was offered a good job in India, her home country, after she finished her Ph.D. at Rotterdam University, but she fell in love with a Dutchman and decided to stay. She married him in 1991 and they now have two children. Rachel works here as a university lecturer, but she goes back to India at least once a year for a lengthy visit to her family.

'It's time to go home. I've really, really enjoyed living here and I'll miss lots of things about Holland. I want to go while I'm still happy here and I know I'll come back and visit friends.'

Marie is about to leave. She came to Holland in 1984, to take up a teaching appointment in an international school. 'I found both the school and Holland very, very easy to settle in to. The school was a small, caring community and everybody bent over backwards to help you. I found Holland a very easy country to live in – after I got over the culture shock of Albert Heijn!' But Marie has decided to go back to Scotland and resigned from her teaching job without a firm job offer to go back to. Why? 'I want to be beside my family now. It's time to go home. I've really, really enjoyed living here and I'll miss lots of things about Holland. I want to go while I'm still happy here and I know I'll come back and visit friends. But I'm totally sure I'm doing the right thing.'

Motoko is also about to leave, to go to England with her partner. She is Japanese and has not found life in Holland easy. She has been working on finishing her doctoral thesis on English literature, which was started at

Cambridge University in England. 'I've been a housewife for the first time! From Monday to Friday I have nobody to speak to. I'm not a very sociable person, I prefer reading, but it's not healthy. I don't belong to any society here. I don't fit in easily. My neighbours are all shopkeepers and I feel guilty that I can't speak Dutch to them.'

Motoko has enjoyed many things about Holland, though. 'Especially compared with Japanese society, Holland is very relaxed. It's clean and shining and the tiny towns are so charming.' But she is looking forward to leaving and to living in an international town in England. 'I'm interested in England, because of my thesis. It will be easier there for me, I hope.'

Ardis is about to leave, after 16 years. She will be sad to leave, yes, but 'I'm ready for a new adventure. It's time to move on now. We'll be closer to our family.' Ardis's last child is about to leave home and go to University. That is often a catalyst for women and families to leave, too.

Wendy likes life in Holland and has a full-time job which she enjoys, but her youngest daughter will go to University in a year's time. 'I don't know if I'll want to stay here for much longer when she's gone – I won't feel the same commitment to Holland then.'

Of course, one problem these happy – and unhappy – leavers create is the unhappy friends they leave behind. When I first came, I met an English woman at an evening class who announced that she had been here for 20 years and now had no friends. 'I've seen so many people come and go that I don't bother making friends any more, because I know they'll just leave.' That may be an extreme and depressing view, but I do have some sympathy. This week I've been to the leaving parties of three women I've been fond of and whom I know I will miss. It is hard to be a long-term resident when so many are just passing through. The other side of the coin is the privilege of having such a wide range of international friendships – and the invitations to California and Malaysia and Aberdeen!

Top ten tips – How to be happy in Holland

1. **Learn Dutch.** Particularly if you have a Dutch partner, of course, or if you plan to stay here long-term. But even if these are not the case, a knowledge of Dutch will help you to feel more at home and give you access to the culture – and a surprising number of women come with the firm intention of staying only for a year and end up still in Holland 10 or 20 years on (or fall in love with a Dutchman after they arrive)!

2. **Ask for help.** Don't sit around puzzled by bureaucracy or at a loss as to where to find what you need. Phone ACCESS, or ask your next-door neighbour, or go to your child's school and say you're stuck. You can always offer help in return, or give a bunch of flowers as a thank-you token. Most people are only too happy to help newcomers – but they don't know what you need until you tell them.

3. **Explore the country.** Get out and about. This is a compact little country with a great public transport network and a glorious collection of museums, art galleries and historic towns. If you can't find anyone to go with, go by yourself. But check out the various expat clubs – they often run excursions to places of interest, with a chartered bus, a guide and good company.

4. **Keep busy.** The devil finds work for idle hands! The devil also has a habit of sowing seeds of doubt and depression in minds that are not profitably occupied. You really will feel much better if you have something specific to do for at least part of the week.

5. **Get involved.** Don't sit on the sidelines, participate. This applies especially if you arrive in the late summer, just before the winter evening classes and activities start in September. If you don't enroll at once, it could be another year before the chance comes round again. You can always cut down on your activities later, once you've decided where your priorities lie. So sign up for Dutch lessons at least, and join a club or two.

6. **Volunteer.** If you don't have a paid job, create one for yourself by volunteering. See chapter 4 for ideas. If you do want a paid job don't settle for just any rubbishy job. There are some truly terrible jobs going, poorly paid and desperately boring. If you can afford to, wait until something more interesting and suitable comes up.

7. **Network.** Make a real effort to meet other women by joining clubs and societies. There are over 80 expat associations in the Netherlands and countless Dutch ones, so there must be one to suit you somewhere.

8. **Find somewhere nice to live.** Make it a priority to find yourself the very best place possible within your budget.

9. **Act as if you're enjoying yourself.** Pretend that this is the best place you've ever been and that you absolutely love it here. (And while you're at it, be kind to yourself, without feeling guilty about it.)

10. **Don't expect to make things the same as they were back home.** It may seem blindingly obvious to say so, but this is Holland and not New York, Paris or London. You will have a much easier time if you accept the differences and go along with them, rather than trying to re-create what you used to have in another life.

Words of wisdom from the women themselves

Most of the women I talked to had some advice to pass on to other women coming to live in Holland. Much of it is already in the text, but here are some of the additional things they said.

On Learning Dutch

Jan: The biggest thing is to try to move into Dutch society a little bit. You can do simple things like joining a small course in Dutch – just get that bridge to cross over. I'm half and half now, Dutch friends and English.

Kate: I'd strongly urge women to learn some Dutch, in order to feel part of the community. Keep persevering. There are some lovely Dutch people out there.

Sue S.: Have Dutch lessons, preferably before you come. Try and make an effort – it really helps. If I'd known about ACCESS before I came it would have been helpful.

Nicole: As a linguist, I say learn Dutch. You can live here very happily without Dutch – living here doesn't encourage it, in fact – but you're at an advantage if you have it. You're not patronised.

Natasha: Show your knowledge and interest in the country. Learn the language – you will **feel** different then – and also the history and the cross-cultural differences. We are guests on a visit here, so make no criticisms. You can make jokes about your own country, but not about this one.

Rachel: Be prepared to speak Dutch. You have to show an openness to understanding Dutch culture and history – for example, the fact that this was a predominantly agricultural society until relatively recently had a major impact. It meant an attitude of respect for the small person and the tolerance (although not necessarily acceptance) of differences.

Hettie: Make the language your first priority – work out a scheme to get a lot of Dutch under your belt before you start working.

Ebe: Learn the language and the history and then you can put up with things that may seem strange. You can absorb the things that you like, but you don't have to do everything the same way as Dutch people. Be open to the country and don't criticise. Take the initiative, be proactive and ask, ask, ask.

Miscellany

Liz: Try and do something for yourself, especially if you have children. People come and go and you lose your friends – you need something to satisfy yourself.

Norma: Don't come with the idea that what you have done is what you are going to do or that it's the only thing you're going to do. Be open to opportunity and make the most of your transferable skills.

Julia O.: You have to make friends quickly and invest yourself or you lose out. If you wait six months to get acclimatised and stay on the sidelines then that's where you'll always be. Jump in with both feet and get involved.

Julia A.: Be who/true to what you are. Develop a support system immediately. Get to know other international women and be prepared to be vulnerable in friendships. Try not to survive but to thrive. This is part of your life that you can't get back, so enjoy it.

Sheila: Get involved with your children's school, or use clubs as a stepping stone to meet other people and learn skills through voluntary work.

Ardis: Don't come with preconceived ideas. Be receptive; take the time to look around and absorb what's here, and then – **after** adjusting – make commitments. Give yourself the gift of time.

Catherine: Be strong and go for what you believe in.

Rosemary: If necessary, ask for help; everyone needs help sometimes. Networking is vital. Once you start setting up a network of contacts, there is incredible support.

Robin: If you have the chance, really talk to people before you come. Seek out women who have already moved, through the Internet.

Lisa: I'd travel around and get to know the place, if you have the time. Take yourself off and wander round The Hague and Amsterdam and soak up the atmosphere. There are some lovely little streets with beautiful architecture and lovely shops. Give yourself time to have a good look round.

Lynne: Sit down with yourself and make a list of your goals. Look at your needs – new needs may surface because you're out of your familiar environment. Being away from home gives you a kind of freedom, so use the time as productively as you can.

Cristina: Do something you've always wanted to do. I had always wanted to try pottery, and the classes I went to opened up a totally different world for me. I also made two good friends there. Most people have a skill or a talent – what can you offer? There is something out there for you. It's up to you what happens to you – no one is going to come and find you.

Christine: You have to make your own opportunities and be proactive. Try to keep up with what is happening in the community at both the national level with daily newspapers and television news and at the local level with the free papers that appear in your letterbox every week.

Ella: The longer you are away from your home country, the more you start treasuring the good memories, until they get out of proportion. Don't always look back. You are here now, so make the best of it.

What makes a successful woman?

While interviewing women for this book, I have pondered about the qualities that enable so many women to overcome obstacles and make a success out of life. All of the women in these pages have faced difficulties of one sort or another in their lives in Holland – don't let their positive outlook fool you into believing that life has all been a bed of roses – yet all have managed to make something better for themselves and other people.

Just as I was nearing my last interview, I read an interview in *The Psychologist* with Michael Howe, Professor of Psychology at Exeter University, about why he studies geniuses. He does not believe that geniuses – he quotes Charlotte Brontë or Marie Curie as examples – are freaks of nature, but rather people who use their experiences and abilities in exceptional ways, which we lesser beings could learn from.

'Geniuses rarely make the mistake of expecting that progress will be easy...Like everyone else, geniuses often encounter difficulties, but when that happens they do not leap to the conclusion that failure is inevitable... They focus their energies on the problems they confront, and keep on persevering, refusing to be distracted by other events or disheartened by their failures.'

It struck me immediately on reading Howe's words that if you substitute '*successful women*' for '*geniuses*' every time it is written, you also get a picture that could be applied to the women in this book. Most will tell you that they have been disheartened at times, of course, but they persevered to overcome their problems and make positive changes.

In other words, don't lose heart and don't give up. You **can** have a happy and successful stay in Holland, like thousands of women before you. Good luck!

Facts and figures

Nationality

15 nationalities are represented:
Australia, Brazil, Canada, Eire, India, Italy, Japan, Luxembourg,
New Zealand, Poland, Russia, South Africa, UK, USA, Zambia

The majority of the women come from the UK or the USA, which is
a reflection of the spread of nationalities in the international expat
community

Children

52% have children living at home
(4 of these are single parents with young children)
18% have no children
30% have children who have left home

Age

90% are aged between 30 and 55

Living

Only 3 live outside the Amsterdam/The Hague area
48% have lived here longer than 10 years
16% have – or have had – a Dutch partner

Work

38% work for an organisation, the majority full-time
44% work freelance and/or have their own business
(of whom half run a fully registered business)
16% have no paid employment
(the missing one is an au pair, working for a family)
22% came to seek or to take up a job in their own right
(of these, 3 women brought a trailing spouse with them)

I make no claims that these women are representative of expat women as a whole, but I do think it interesting that 84% are in some kind of employment, be it only occasional freelance work.

N.B. In case you add up the women mentioned in the book and don't reach 50, you need to know that there are some doubles:

Two Sues – ACCESS volunteer and runner
Two Rachels – young oil company worker and University lecturer
Two Jeans – art teacher and aerobics fan
Two Julias – coach and computer expert
Two Kates – medical audit officer and magazine contributor
Two Jans – stained glass artist and embassy information librarian
One Jennie – New Zealand Embassy
One Jenny – Brownie leader
One Marie – about to leave
One Mharie – taking a poetry course

Resources
Reference List

Books and magazines about Holland

- *An ABC of the Netherlands* by Suzanne Wensink
  (A Dutch primer for children)
- *A Curious Landscape: Foreign Writers on The Netherlands*
  by Gwynne and Peter van Zonneveld
- *An Irishman's Difficulties with the Dutch Language* by Cuey-na-Gael
- *Babies and Toddlers: the ACCESS Guide to having Children in Holland*
  published by ACCESS
- *At Home in Holland* published by The American Women's Club
- *Dutch Cooking* by Heleen Halverhout
- *Dutch Cooking Today* published by Immerc B.V.
- *The Flavour of Holland* by Hilary Keating
- *Food Shoppers' Guide to Holland* by Ada Henne Koene
- *Health Care in Holland* published by ACCESS
- *Here's Holland* by Sheila Gazaleh-Weevers
- *The Holland Handbook* published by XPat Media
- *Inside Information* by Caroline Gelderman
- *Live and Work in Belgium, The Netherlands and Luxembourg*
  by André de Vries
- *The Low Sky* by Han van der Horst
- *The Low Sky in Pictures* by Han van der Horst
- *The Netherlands Cookbook* by Heleen Halverhout
- *The Simple Guide to Holland: Customs and Etiquette* by Mark T.Hooker

The ACCESS Newsletter (tel. 070 - 346 25 25)
Expats Magazine

Roundabout
The XPat Journal

ACCESS offers a welcome package of publications for expats at
70 euros per pack.

Booksellers

www.abc.nl (American Book Store)
www.access-nl.org
www.amazon.co.uk
www.deslegte.nl (de Slegte bookstore)
www.nl.bol.com (books online, Dutch site)

General expat books and magazines

- *Culture Shock: A Student's Guide* by Robert Barlas and Guek-Cheng Pang
- *Hidden Immigrants: Legacies of Growing Up Abroad* by Linda Bell
- *Homeward Bound: A Spouse's Guide to Repatriation* by Robin Pascoe
- *Living and Working Abroad: A Parent's Guide* by Robin Pascoe
- *Living and Working Abroad: A Wives' Guide* by Robin Pascoe
- *Third Culture Kids* by David Pollack and Ruth van Reken

Robin Pascoe has her own website at www.expatexpert.com
Woman Abroad magazine & website (www.womanabroad.com)

Websites for expats

www.access-nl.org
www.britain.nl (British Embassy site)
www.elynx.nl
www.expatexchange.com
www.expatica.com
www.expatsonline.nl
www.expatspouse.com

www.juliaferguson.com
www.mumsabroad.com
www.outpostexpat.nl
www.womanabroad.com
www.xpat.nl

Clubs and societies

www.aatg.nl (Anglo-American Theatre Group)
www.britishsocietyofamsterdam.org
www.bwclubthehague.demon.nl (British Women's Club)
www.connectingwomen.nl
www.foreignfriends.nl
www.rickross.com/groups/landmark.html
www.scooponlandmarkforum.com

Careers books and websites

- *Build Your Own Rainbow. A Handbook for Career and Life Management* by Hopson & Scally
- *The Complete Idiot's Guide to Changing Careers* by William Charland
- *Do What You Are* by Paul Tieger and Barbara Barron-Tieger
- *How to Set Up and Run Your Own Business* by Helen Kogan
- *Is There A Book Inside You?* By Dan Poynter and Mandy Bingham
- *The Perfect cv* by Tom and Ella Jackson
- *The SEED Handbook: The Feminine Way to Create a Business* by Lynne Franks
- *What Color is Your Parachute?: A Practical Manual for Job-Hunters and Career Changers* by Richard Nelson

Amazon has a *Choosing a Career* list on its website, www.amazon.co.uk

www.b&n.com (Barnes and Noble 'university')
www.queendom.com (careers, aptitude and personality tests)

Jobsearch websites

http://missions.itu.int/~italy/vacancies
(vacancies in international organisations)
www.adamsrecruit.nl
www.adecco.nl
www.bluelynx.nl
www.dacumac.nl
www.elsevier.nl
www.englishlanguagejobs.nl
www.esa.int (European Space Agency)
www.expatica.com
www.info.nld.chello.nl
www.jobnews.nl
www.kellyservices.nl
www.lady.co.uk (au pairs and nannies)
www.monsterboard.nl
www.newscientistjobs.com
www.open.ac.uk
www.ripe.net
www.shell.com/careers-en
www.stepstone.nl
www.undutchables.nl
www.uniquemls.com

Education in Holland

www.counselling.nl/cpcab.html
www.linguarama.nl (Dutch teaching)
www.nti.nl (Dutch teaching)
www.nuffic.nl
www.reginacoeli.nl (Dutch teaching)
www.sio.nl (list of all international schools)
www.uu.nl (University of Utrecht)
www.webster.nl

Distance learning

www.bn.com
www.bsygroup.co.uk (British School of Yoga)
www.cheltenhamlearning.co.uk
www.collegeofcounselling.com
www.icdl.open.ac.uk (register of distance courses worldwide)
www.nec.ac.uk (National Extension College)
www.olionline.com (TEFL training courses)
www.oca-uk.com (Open College of the Arts)
www.open.ac.uk (Open University)

Making a website

www.pdnl.nl
www.domain-registry.nl
www.geocities.yahoo.com
www.homestead.com
www.domeinplaza.nl
www.uk2net.com

Family History

* *Our Family Tree Record Book* published by Dorling Kindersley
* *Our Family History: Record Book, Photograph Album and Family Tree* published by The Reader's Digest
* *Kids Love Travel Memories. A Family Keepsake Book for Scrapbooking All the Fun Places You' ve Visited* by George Zavatsky.

www.spansoft.org
www.familysearch.org

Culture, travel and friendships in Holland

www.a-t-c.demon.nl (American Travel Center)
www.ceciliamusic.nl
www.studiojean.nl
www.mycruiseferries.nl

Shopping in Holland

www.darling.nl (Darling Market)
www.neckermann.nl (catalogue shopping)
www.tefaf.com (The European Fine Art Fair)
www.xotus.nl (exotic garden centre)

Miscellaneous

www.allabouteve.beeb.com (magazine)
www.animalfreedom.org
www.coachfederation.org
www.coachville.com
www.dmoz.org (web directory)
www.doctorbackhome.com
www.mindpixel.com (teaching computer to think)
www.nvm.nl (Dutch real estate site)
www.proefdiervrij.nl (against animal testing)
www.talesmag.com (travel stories)
www.upledger.nl (alternative health)
www.vistapapers.co.uk (office stationery)

The Aurora Center for Natural Medicine and Personal Growth in
Amsterdam (Herengracht 607, tel.: 020 - 421 19 87)
The Hague Support Group for parents of handicapped children.
Cathy Hart is the contact person, tel.: 070 - 317 51 01;
e-mail hotcitygirl@hotmail.com

Colophon

Text
Janet Inglis
Editing
Stephanie Dijkstra
Graphic design
Marlies Bredie (Manifesta), Rotterdam
Cover design
Paul Weijs
Printing
Snoeck-Ducaju & Zoon, Gent
Publisher
XPAT MEDIA